JAN 8 1985

Regulation of Direct Broadcasting from Satellites

Benno Signitzer

The Praeger Special Studies program—utilizing the most modern and efficient book production techniques and a selective worldwide distribution network—makes available to the academic, government, and business communities significant, timely research in U.S. and international economic, social, and political development.

Regulation of Direct
Broadcasting from Satellites
The UN Involvement

PRAEGER SPECIAL STUDIES IN INTERNATIONAL POLITICS AND GOVERNMENT

Praeger Publishers   New York   Washington   London

Library of Congress Cataloging in Publication Data

Signitzer, Benno.
    Regulation of direct broadcasting from satellites.

    (Praeger special studies in international politics
and government)
    Bibliography: p.
    Includes index.
    1. Artificial satellites in telecommunication.
2. United Nations. I. Title.
HE9719.S5   341.7'577   76-14372
ISBN 0-275-56800-8

PRAEGER PUBLISHERS
111 Fourth Avenue, New York, N.Y. 10003, U.S.A.

Published in the United States of America in 1976
by Praeger Publishers, Inc.

Printed in the United States of America

The emergence of the direct broadcast satellite (DBS) constitutes a revolutionary development in modern communications technology. While traditional satellite communication systems, such as those employed by the International Telecommunications Satellite Organization (INTELSAT) or by Intersputnik, require big and sophisticated earth stations, the direct broadcast satellite will be able to send the signals directly to the home of the receiver. In other terms, what was possible in the past only with shortwave radio—the beaming of messages across national boundaries directly to a global audience—will be technologically feasible with television.

It is the prospect of a visual Voice of America or Radio Moscow that accounts for the politically explosive nature of this new technology. Expressions of both anxiety and hope, at times exaggerated, have been indicative of the debate on DBS that has been under way since the late 1960s. The fears refer to possible abuse of DBS for propaganda purposes, invasion of cultural privacy, and the destruction of vulnerable local economies. On the other hand, great hopes have been expressed with respect to DBS's tremendous educational and nation-building potential. In fall 1975, for instance, the National Aeronautics and Space Administration's (NASA's) ATS-6 (Application Technology Satellite) began broadcasting instructional TV programs directly to community receivers in 5,000 Indian villages. A single satellite will easily cover the whole subcontinent. The advantages of cost saving and efficiency over traditional—terrestrial—broadcasting are obvious.

Ever since the feasibility of this new technology became apparent, questions of policy and regulation have been posed by proponents and opponents alike. The whole range of issues that characterize domestic debates on communications policy—freedom of speech, censorship, fairness, access, to name only a few—has acquired global dimensions. The United Nations Committee on the Peaceful Uses of Outer Space (Outer Space Committee) has become the focal point for these wide-ranging policy discussions. Similarly, the International Telecommunication Union (ITU) has concerned itself with technical questions surrounding DBS while UNESCO has concentrated on educational and cultural issues, especially as they apply to the emerging nations. In view of possible regulation, direct satellite broadcasting has been regarded as a space activity against the background of the emerging law of outer space. This study will concentrate on political and regulatory problems of DBS as they have manifested themselves within the United Nations in general and the Outer Space Committee in particular.

The principal aims of this study are twofold:
1. to trace the history and current status of the UN involvement in the ordering of the direct broadcast satellite

2. to analyze this political and legislative process within the UN Outer Space Committee, to establish the relative positions of the member countries on a free flow–control continuum, and to relate the findings to other variables

In order to establish the conceptual framework in which DBS is embedded, Chapter 1 will describe briefly origin and technical preconditions in presently existing systems of satellite communications as well as their organizational setup. The chapter will provide an assessment of the most important definitional and technical parameters involved in direct broadcasting by satellites as well as a brief overview of pertinent questions relating to the regulation of spectrum and orbit, patterns of utilization, and planned systems of DBS.

Chapter 2 will be dealing with some basic principles of the emerging law of space communications.

Chapter 3, then, will present a rather detailed account of the increasing involvement of the United Nations and the Outer Space Committee in the issues of DBS. It will describe what could be called the making of the issue during 1963-68; and will deal with the evolution of the question within the committee's Working Group on Direct Broadcast Satellites (1969-74) and its legal subcommittee (1974-75) as well as with the General Assembly debate of 1972 that proved crucial for further developments.

Finally, Chapter 4's concern will be with the abovementioned questions connected with free flow versus control and legislative versus operational approach models, which in turn leads to the conclusions in Chapter 5.

ACKNOWLEDGMENTS

This book would not have been possible without the generous help and encouragement that I have received from many sources. I wish to express my gratitude to the following:

To Professors David Clark, Malachi Topping, and Harold Fisher of Bowling Green State University whose warm support and encouragement greatly enriched my studies in the United States. This book evolved from my Ph.D. thesis written under their direction and guidance; to the Austrian-American Educational Commission (Fulbright Commission), Vienna, which supported my initial efforts to come to the United States; to the Research Services Office, Bowling Green State University, which provided financial support for my research at the United Nations; to Mr. Alexander Christiani from the Austrian Mission to the United Nations and Mr. Johan Lind from the Swedish Mission to the United Nations for their generous help and advice during my work at the United Nations; to Mrs. Ita Pasztor and Mr. M. W. Robinson from the Outer Space Affairs Division, United Nations, for guiding me in the use of their excellent library facilities and making available documentary materials; and to Mr. Bert Cowlan, consultant, and Mr. Frederick Hartley, U.S. Department of State. My discussions with them provided invaluable insights and perspective.

CONTENTS

LIST OF TABLES

Ever since the space age began with Sputnik I in 1957, the United Nations has shown an extraordinary interest in man's activities in outer space. As early as 1959, the General Assembly set up a permanent committee, the UN Committee on the Peaceful Uses of Outer Space (Outer Space Committee), to deal exclusively with the implications of space technology. This committee has been instrumental in the creation of what came to be known as space law. Numerous General Assembly resolutions on the peaceful uses of outer space set forth some basic principles such as "free use," "sovereign equality of states," "prohibition of national appropriation," "common heritage of all mankind," and so on. These efforts culminated in the Outer Space Treaty of 1967, which is a cornerstone of the law of outer space.

There are two basic schools of thought on ways of coping with technological advancement. One approach favors the greatest possible freedom for technological development—unhampered by restrictions and regulations. Laws and policies, it is contended, should result from a body of experience with the effects of innovation. The other school of thought asserts the primacy of policy over technology; a certain amount of regulation should precede new technology and guide the course of its development.

The history of the UN concern with outer space suggests that the latter approach has been taken. This is not to say, however, that this dichotomy that juxtaposes regulation and innovation has been totally resolved in favor of regulation. Indeed, this conflict is at the very heart of the issue of DBS.

As a result, partly of the successful conclusion of the space treaty, partly of the great attention feasibility studies of the direct broadcast satellite (DBS) received at the UN Outer Space Conference held at Vienna, in 1968, the General Assembly, in Resolution 2453, requested the Outer Space Committee to establish a Working Group on Direct Broadcast Satellites. According to the resolution, the committee was to study and report on the technical feasibility of communication by direct broadcast from satellites and the current and foreseeable developments in this field, "including comparative user costs and other economic considerations, as well as the implications of such developments in the social, cultural, legal and other areas."

The working group has met five times: twice in 1969, once in 1970, 1973, and 1974. The last meeting produced several drafts on principles governing the use of direct broadcast satellites which were referred to the Legal Subcommittee of the Outer Space Committee that has met on DBS in 1974 and in February 1975. The Outer Space Committee as well as its subcommittees are presently composed of 37 nations representing all the major powers and regions of the world.

METHODOLOGY AND SOURCES

This study will trace the history of the UN concern with DBS and UN attempts at establishing a framework of order within which this new technology should operate. The main emphasis will be on the period 1969 through 1975 that witnessed an intensification of these efforts. During this time the abovementioned meetings of the working group and of the legal subcommittee generated the following source material:

1. General Assembly resolutions, working papers, committee reports.
2. Verbatim and summary records.
3. Unofficial statements by delegations.
4. UN press releases.
5. Personal letters received from delegations.
6. Personal interviews with delegations conducted at the United Nations, New York, February 20-March 6, 1975.
7. Personal observations and notes, taken at the February 15-March 7, 1975 meeting of the legal subcommittee.

The following nations are represented in the Outer Space Committee and all its subsidiary bodies:

1. Original members: Albania, Australia, Austria, Belgium, Brazil, Bulgaria, Canada, Chad, Czechoslovakia, Egypt, France, Hungary, India, Iran, Italy, Japan, Lebanon, Mexico, Mongolia, Morocco, Poland, Romania, Sierra Leone, Sweden, USSR, United Kingdom, United States.
2. New members (since 1973): Chile, German Democtratic Republic, Federal Republic of Germany, Indonesia, Kenya, Nigeria, Pakistan, Sudan, Venezuela.

The information available will be examined at the following levels: (1) the nature of the international process itself; (2) the free flow-control continuum; (3) trend analysis, 1969-75.

The following hypothesis will be explored: an embryonic international legislative process is emerging; the Outer Space Committee is playing the role of parliamentary standing committees and the General Assembly that of a parliament—albeit one whose acts must be ratified by the governments of members.[1] In procedural terms A. E. Gotlieb and C. M. Dalfen discerned a pattern consisting of three stages: (1) committee work (plus subcommittees, working groups, reports); (2) General Assembly resolutions; (3) conclusion of conventions. The purpose of this analysis is to test and expand the legislative process model through examination of the events that contributed to the making of the issue (1963-69) and of the current state of affairs.

This approach is based on the assumption that the concepts of free flow and control, however rough, can define the end points of a continuum between which all countries can be positioned. This continuum will be established in the light of later developments—especially with regard to the results of the meeting of the legal subcommittee, February 15 to March 7, 1975. In order to facilitate classification of the positions of the states their delegations' views on a few key issues will be examined.

An attempt will be made to identify shifts of positions in the period under study with respect to both policy stands of the member countries and changes in the nature of the committee work itself. The material available will be discussed in the light of another pair of categories, legislative versus operational approach: the former involves the positing of norms and rules while the latter advocates their development on the basis of actual practice. The former draws on norms and analogies in other areas of international law while the latter focuses on the activity itself and on its own particular technology.[2] These philosophic differences have to do with culture, legal tradition (Latin versus Anglo-Saxon law), and level of political and economic development.

PREVIOUS UN WRITINGS ON DIRECT SATELLITE BROADCASTING

As is apparent from the Bibliography, there is ample literature on space law in general, on existing systems of satellite communications (the U.S. Communications Satellite Corporation [COMSAT], INTELSAT, and so on), and on selected legal and political aspects of the direct broadcast satellite. However, scholarly thought on the narrower subject of this study, the political and legislative treatment of DBS within the UN Outer Space Committee, is still at an embryonic stage.

A first attempt at organizing the wealth of documentaty UN materials around a conceptual framework was made by Gotlieb and Dalfen; both in structural and processual terms, they discern a pattern in the making of new international law governing technological innovation within the UN system. They define the function and purpose of the General Assembly and the respective committees (structure) and, as noted previously, describe the various stages of their work (process): (1) committee discussion, study, and recommendation; (2) assembly resolution, and (3) the conclusion of an international convention.

Dalfen refines and extends the above approach.[3] He applies it to other areas such as remote earth sensing and introduces the previously explained legislative versus operational approach variable which enables him to account for shifts in the process.

Ithiel de Sola Pool's application of the traditional freedom-control continuum to DBS, then, opens the way for qualitative assessments of member countries' positions as well as the process itself.[4]

NOTES

1. A. E. Gotlieb and C. M. Dalfen, "Direct Satellite Broadcasting: A Case Study in the Development of the Law of Space Communications," Canadian Yearbook of International Law 7 (1969): pp. 33-60 (hereafter cited as "Case Study").

2. Charles M. Dalfen, "The International Legislative Process: Direct Broadcasting and Remote Earth Sensing by Satellites Compared," Canadian Yearbook of International Law 11 (1973): pp. 186-211 (hereafter "DBS and Remote Sensing Compared").

3. Ibid.

4. Ithiel de Sola Pool, "Direct Satellites and the Integrity of National Cultures," in Aspen Institute, Control of the Direct Broadcast Satellite. Values in Conflict (Palo Alto: Aspen Institute, 1974), pp. 27-36 (hereafter cited as Values in Conflict).

**COMMUNICATIONS
BY SATELLITE**

ORIGINS AND TECHNICAL PRECONDITIONS

There is a consensus among media historians to trace the history
of communication satellites to a definite moment in time and to a definite moment in time and to a definite individual. In October 1945 Arthur
C. Clarke, a young British radio expert and science writer, published
a prophetic article entitled "The Future of World Communications."[1]
In this article, Clarke introduced the idea of combining rocketry and
microwave engineering to provide artificial satellites in stationary orbits
around the earth serving as relays for transmissions from earth. He
noted that "many may consider the solution proposed in this discussion
too far-fetched to be taken very seriously. Such an attitude is unrea-
sonable as everything envisaged here is a logical extension of developments in the last ten years—in particular the perfection of the long-
range rocket of which V-2 was the prototype."[2]
It took some time before Clarke's idea was recognized and, then,
in a different way from what he had imagined. Experiments using artificial satellites could not begin until the beginning of the space age
in the late 1950s. Some of these experiments were an outgrowth of the
use of the moon as a reflector. The orbit of the moon is anything but
ideal for communication between various points on earth. But with
metallized balloons launched by rockets to sufficient altitude and
placed in orbit around earth, and adequate ground installations for
transmission and reception, a passive satellite communication system
became possible. This concept was realized through the highly successful U.S. project Echo I which was launched in August 1960 and
used for relay of telephony, facsimile, and other data.[3] This so-called
passive satellite type had various disadvantages, above all, the in-
efficient use of transmission power. As new, miniaturized electronic
equipment made it possible to launch remote-controlled transmitters,

experiments were undertaken with satellites that carried on-board radio communication equipment for the reception, amplification, and retransmission of messages received from earth. The advantages of such active satellites have proved so superior to the passive type that developments have concentrated almost exclusively on the active kind of satellite.[4]

These early experiments had to determine such factors as the optimum selection of spacecraft subsystems, altitude control, station keeping, power supply, antenna design, telemetry, and command and control for operational use in an earth/space environment. They did prove the feasibility of the idea.[5] In June 1962, experiments had already started on a major scale with the Telstar and Relay satellites for intercontinental, wideband communications, including television transmissions. "Within a few years, development had progressed from the use of the large balloon-type reflectors to sophisticated active repeaters.[6] And already at this early stage, it became obvious that satellite systems could provide a capacity and flexibility which would make them a focal point for the development of international communications. Progress was rapid. Satellite communication may be said to have passed through an "experimental period lasting about five years, followed by an initial utilization period which now has resulted in full operational status."[7]

It is important to note that these early efforts in the development of space (communications) technology were not solely determined by technical considerations. The celebrated space race between the Soviet Union and the United States provided the political and psychological background for these operations. It seems possible that some of the ideological disputes that have surrounded the application of this technology are rooted in the competitive character of its early development.

A satellite communication system came to be understood to comprise both the satellite itself with the necessary control and tracking facilities (space segments) and the associated earth stations (ground or earth segment). In addition to differences stemming from active versus passive satellites, there are also substantial operational differences depending on the altitude and orientation of orbit of the satellites.

Low- and Medium-Altitude Satellites

A medium- or low-altitude system, orbiting at 6,000 to 12,000 miles, requires the use of several satellites for global coverage, plus elaborate scanning, tracking, and high-powered receiving equipment. Each satellite is within the line of sight or view of a particular pair of transmitting and receiving stations only for a comparatively short time before it is hidden by the curvature of the earth. To maintain continuous communication, a second satellite must be in the view of the pair of stations before the first satellite passes from view below the horizon. Thus, a medium-altitude system may require a dozen or more satellites to insure visibility between pairs of stations most of the time.[8]

Synchronous Satellites

An alternative to the low- and medium-altitude satellite system is the high-orbiting synchronous equatorial satellite. A synchronous satellite is placed approximately 22,300 miles above the equator and revolves around the earth at a speed synchronized with the rotation of the earth. Thus the satellite appears to be in a stationary position above a point on the earth, making it possible to utilize slightly less expensive but nonetheless complicated scanning and tracking equipment.[9] In the synchronous system one satellite is able to cover 160 degrees of the globe but cannot cover either of the polar caps. The system requires only three satellites to provide satisfactory worldwide coverage, but each requires a precise separate launch by a more powerful booster than that required for the lower altitude satellites.[10]

Other operational advantages have been realized. The fixed location and orientation of such satellites allow for the use of highly directive (focused) antennas capable of producing more powerful coverage of a selected area of the earth's surface. Frequency sharing between earth stations and terrestrial radio relay stations thus became much more feasible.[11]

Another method for coverage of extremely northern or southern latitudes which cannot easily be reached from the synchronous, equatorial orbit, consists in launching satellites into orbits that are elliptical and very eccentric in the sense that the highest point of the orbit (apogee) is above the area to be covered. These satellites are of the type used by the Soviet Union (as described below) to cover, for 10-12 hours continuously, the entire Soviet territory including the northernmost parts.[12]

Quite a different pattern of use is being introduced with the various various forms of direct broadcast satellite systems. In this case, television (or sound radio) programs transmitted from an earth station to a powerful satellite will be broadcast from the satellite for reception by individual receivers, without the need for intermediate earth stations. This system and its regulation represent the subject matter of the present study; this chapter will describe in some detail its technical and operational conditions.

UNESCO, in a study, then, summarizes the main characteristics of satellite communication systems:

A. Flexibility. The advantage lies in the satellite system's multiple route capacity as opposed to the single route capability of terrestrial systems. Through satellite communication facilities, it is possible to serve multiple routes through a single facility and of reallocating channel capacity among these routes. Thus, in addition to point-to-point communication between pairs of earth stations, it is possible to provide point-to-multiple-point trans- missions from one earth station to a number of earth stations which can be activated and deactivated at will without affecting the overall system.

B. Capacity. Satellite systems can furnish previously impossible broadband services as proven by transoceanic television transmissions which could not be handled through terrestrial means. In principle, communication satellites may be used for any kind of electronic communication services.

C. Geographical Coverage and Cost. Inherent in satellite communications is the capability to provide in- terconnections over very large distances and to cover wide areas of the surface of the earth. The cost of a link be- tween the two earth stations via satellite is largely inde- pendent of the distance separating them, so that, at least in theory there need be no substantial difference between long-haul and short-haul traffic.[13]

The UNESCO study also lists some disadvantages of satellite communication systems that have been specifically discussed:

The further demands on the already heavily committed frequency spectrum and the risk of interference with ter- restrial systems;
The hitherto limited operational life-time of satellites which goes from five to ten years;
Greater vulnerability and sensitivity to interference than terrestrial systems.[14]

As to this last point, however, some of these disadvantages are already in the process of being overcome.

EXISTING SYSTEMS OF SATELLITE COMMUNICATION

Satellite communications facilities may be organized and owned on a national or international basis, and ownership may be public, private, or mixed. Political pressures and national policies continue to exercise at least as much influence on the communications structure as the legal, economic, and technological factors.[15] It is, therefore, hardly surprising that the two main existing satellite communication systems for telecommunication traffic are rather dissimilar in terms of technical solutions and objectives.

One of these systems, the International Telecommunications Satellite Organization (INTELSAT), has been established to provide international, mainly intercontinental, communications links and uses geostationary satellites and large, elaborate earth stations connected to the national telecommunication networks.[16] Membership in INTELSAT requires accession by a government to the system's agreement among governments and the signing of the companion operating agreement by a government or its designated public or private telecommunications entity. The two agreements, known collectively as the definitive agreements, entered into force on February 12, 1973, superseding an earlier interim agreement of 1964. INTELSAT membership is open to any state that was a party to the interim agreements and to any other state that is a member of the International Telecommunication Union (ITU). As of February 1976, INTELSAT had 92 members.[17]

The satellites of the global system and associated ground control equipment, known as the space segment, are owned by INTELSAT. Each signatory to the operating agreement has an investment share in INTELSAT equal to its percentage use of the system. Representation on the board of governors, the governing body of INTELSAT, is available to any signatory to the operating agreement, or group of signatories with an investment share equal to the minimum level established annually by the meeting of signatories. This minimum, presently 1.11 percent, automatically qualifies all signatories with equal or greater investment shares for representation on the board of governors. Investment shares for the 14 countries which in 1974 automatically qualified were as follows: the United States (38.5 percent), the United Kingdom (10.4), Japan (4.9), France (4.4), Germany (3.6), Canada (3.4), Australia (3.1), Italy (2.8), Spain (2.7), Brazil (1.8), Argentina (1.7), Israel (1.5), Switzerland (1.4), and Greece (1.1).[18] Distinctly different ownership arrangements apply to the satellites and the earth stations in the global system. While the satellites are owned by the 92-nation INTELSAT organization, the earth stations are individually owned by designated telecommunications entities in the respective countries. As of February 1976, the worldwide network of earth stations working with the satellites over the Atlantic, Pacific, and Indian oceans had grown to 130 antennas at 104 station sites in 71 countries.[19]

While in the United States a special body, the U.S. Communications Satellite Corporation (COMSAT), has been set up for the purpose of international communications via satellites, in most other countries this activity is handled by those bodies traditionally in charge of telecommunications: telecommunication administrations, ministries of communication, recognized telecommunication carriers, and so on.[20]

COMSAT functions as the manager of INTELSAT. It was created by the Communications Satellite Act of 1962 that provides for a privately

owned corporation. The act was passed by a large majority over the
opposition of a few vocal members of Congress who insisted that
communications utilizing space should be a government operation.
Arguments advanced were that the public through a government operation should receive the benefits of the enormous space research and
development costs; that most other states treated communications as
a government monopoly; and that international negotiations might be
expedited if a government agency handled the matter for the United
States.[21] The United States, however, has ordinarily followed the rule
that private enterprise should be favored except where national security
is involved or where it is evident that private enterprise is unable or
unwilling to act.[22] In this case it was argued that a private, profit-
oriented, commercial system for U.S. participation in INTELSAT offered
substantial advantages, especially greater efficiency and greater private investment.[23]

Nevertheless, the Communications Satellite Act provides for ex-
tensive supervision, guidance, control of, and aid to, COMSAT by
the president, Congress, the National Aeronautics and Space Administration, the attorney general, the Federal Communications Commission,
and the Department of State.[24] The impact of satellite communications
systems on international affairs is recognized, and the president is
directed to

> . . . Exercise such supervision over relationships of
> the corporation with foreign governments or entities or
> with international bodies as may be appropriate to assure
> that such relationships shall be consistent with the na-
> tional interest and foreign policy of the United States;
> . . . Insure that timely arrangements are made under
> which there can be foreign participation in the establish-
> ment and use of a communications satellite system;
> . . . So exercise his authority as to help attain co-
> ordinated and efficient use of the electromagnetic spec-
> trum and the technical compatibility of the system with
> existing communication facilities both in the United
> States and abroad.[25]

The second main satellite communication system, the Intersputnik system, by contrast, is based on the USSR domestic satellite system
called Orbita which uses larger satellites of the Molnya type in elliptical, highly eccentric orbits around the earth, providing coverage
of the whole national territory.[26] A preliminary draft agreement on
the establishment of Intersputnik was adopted by representatives of
Bulgaria, Cuba, Czechoslovakia, the German Democratic Republic,
Hungary, Mongolia, Poland, Romania, and the Soviet Union at a conference held in Budapest in May 1968. The intergovernmental agreement on the establishment of Intersputnik as an international space

communication system and organization was signed in Moscow on November 15, 1971.[27] Intersputnik is an international organization open to states whose governments have signed the agreement or acceded to it. The system comprises (1) a space segment consisting of communication satellites and terrestrial guidance systems which are the property of all the members; and (2) earth stations which are built by the member countries on their own territory and with their own resources, and are the property of the states operating them.[28]

The main governing organ of Intersputnik is its board, composed of one representative from each member state. Each representative has one vote. The board considers all questions of general policy and principle affecting the activities of the organization, its fundamental lines of development, and other matters within the scope of the functions stipulated by the agreement.[29] Intersputnik is financed from a statutory fund made up on a pro rata basis of members' contributions, the size of which is determined by the extent to which they use the communication channels provided.[30]

THE DIRECT BROADCAST SATELLITE

[Existing communication satellite systems serve broadcasters in two ways: One is by transmitting broadcast programs over great distances between large earth stations, which are linked through terrestrial transmission networks to national program originating and/or distribution centers. The second is by relaying broadcast programs over large distances to medium-sized earth stations connected to local service broadcast transmitters for subsequent rebroadcast of the program in the immediate region.

Direct broadcasting from satellites (DBS) implies the elimination of earth stations and rebroadcast transmitters and the reception of the satellite signal on individual receiving sets.] For radio broadcasting, the introduction of the direct satellite would not create significant new problems in terms of technical regulation or control of program content for existing conventional systems already broadcast over very long ranges. The international community has been living with the problems of interference, propaganda, and protection of program content created by the ability of national broadcasting entities to transmit their programs at long range across state lines.[31]

For television, however, the advent of the direct broadcast satellite has an entirely different significance.[32] Because of the propagation characteristics of television signals that confine their reach to a short radius around the transmitter, television broadcasting to date has been largely a domestic affar unless special arrangements are made as in the case of Eurovision and Intervision:

> International problems created by harmful inter-
> ference or offensive program content have not been
> acute, are confined to areas along the boundary bet-
> ween two states, and are thus primarily bilateral in
> character. These insulating conditions dissolve with
> the introduction of satellite repeaters in synchronous
> orbit.[33]

With such a system, it will be possible for the first time for a single
sending station to broadcast its television programs around the globe,
without the interposition of any externally controlled linkages between
it and the terrestrial receivers. The synchronous satellite opens up the
same capability for television broadcasting that has existed until now
for powerful shortwave radio transmitters, with the added factors of the
decisive impact of the television medium and the much higher quality
of the satellite signal.[34]

In 1969, the UN Working Group on Direct Broadcast Satellites
reached the following conclusions with regard to the feasibility of
satellite broadcasting:

> While it is considered that satellite technology has
> reached the stage at which it is possible to contemplate
> the future development of satellites capable of direct
> broadcasting to the public at large, direct broadcasting
> television into existing unaugmented home receivers
> on an operational basis is not foreseen for the period
> 1970-1985.
>
> Direct broadcast of television into augmented home
> receivers could become feasible technologically as soon
> as 1975. However, the cost factors for both the earth and
> space segments of such a system are inhibiting factors.
>
> Direct broadcasting into community receivers could
> be close at hand. Technology currently under develop-
> ment might allow this in the mid-1970's. Such a system
> is considered to be less expensive to launch than one
> intended for reception directly into people's homes
> [author's emphasis].[35]

These categories correspond roughly to the definitions of three grades
of broadcast satellite services proposed by the International Radio
Consultive Committee (CCIR) of the ITU:

> Primary (Principal) Grade of Service. A grade of service
> such that a power-flux density of sufficient magnitude to
> enable the general public to receive transmissions directly
> from the satellites by means of individual installations and
> with a quality comparable to that provided by a terrestrial
> transmitter to its primary service areas.

Secondary (Rural) Grade of Service. A grade of service
with a lower power-flux density than that required for a
primary grade of service, the signals of which are intended
for direct public reception from satellites by means of individual installations and with an acceptable quality in
sparsely populated areas which are not served, or are in-
adequately served, by other means and where satellite
reception conditions are favourable.
Community Grade of Service. A Grade of broadcasting
service from satellites with a limited power-flux density,
the signals of which are intended for group viewing or
listening or for reception by a master receiver installation.[36]

When the World Administrative Radio Conference for Space Telecommunications met in Geneva in 1971, it adopted the following definitions for satellite broadcasting.

Broadcasting satellite service, is defined as "a radiocommunication service in which signals transmitted or retransmitted by space
stations are intended for direct reception by the general public." This
definition is complemented with a footnote stating: "In the broadcasting-
satellite service, the term direct reception shall encompass both individual reception and community reception."[37] Individual reception
is "the reception of emissions from a space station in the broadcasting
satellite service by simple domestic installations and in particular
those possessing small antennas."[38] Community reception is the reception of emissions from a space station in the broadcasting satellite
service by receiving equipment, which in some cases may be complex
and have antennas larger than those used for individual reception. Community reception is intended for use either by a group of the general
public at one location, or through a distribution system covering a
limited area.[39]

Some Technical Questions in Direct
Satellite Broadcasting

A rigorous assessment of all the technical parameters involved
in DBS would be impractical within the context of this study. Consequently, the following discussion will cover only the most important
parameters, that is, those which have a more direct and immediate
bearing on the practical choice of a direct broadcast satellite system.[40]

Choice of Orbit

The choice of orbit for satellite broadcasting is influenced primarily by the coverage required and the daily hours of transmission desired. A satellite in the geostationary orbit would allow coverage to individual countries using spot beams and continental coverage with global beams. Transmission time could probably be continuous, assuming sufficient power was available on the satellite. A limitation of geostationary satellites is that coverage beyond 70 degrees of latitude north or south is not effective. Polar area coverage could be provided by nonsynchronous satellites in high elliptical orbits although they could require more elaborate receiving antennas.[41] Overall it can be concluded that the geostationary orbit has considerable advantages and therefore no further consideration is usually given to nonsynchronous satellites.

Frequencies

In 1971, the World Administrative Radio Conference (WARC) for Space Telecommunications convened by the ITU allocated frequency bands to the satellite broadcasting service. The frequency allocations are as follows.

Within the frequency band 620-790 MHz, assignments may be made to television stations using frequency modulation in the broadcasting satellite service. These assignments are subject to agreement between administrations concerned and those having services, operating in accordance with the table of frequency allocations in the ITU's radio regulations, which may be affected.[42]

The use of frequency band 2500-2690 MHz by the broadcasting satellite service is limited to domestic and regional systems for community reception and such use is subject to agreement between the administrations concerned and those having services operating in accordance with the table of frequency allocations, which may be affected.[43]

In the frequency band 11.7-12.5 GHz in region A (America) and in the band 11.7-12.5 GHz in region A, existing and future fixed, mobile, and broadcasting services must not cause harmful interference to broadcasting satellite stations operating in accordance with the decisions of the appropriate broadcasting assignment planning conference.[44]

In the band 11.7-12.2 GHz in regions A and B (Western Europe) use by the broadcasting satellite and fixed satellite services is limited to domestic systems and is subject to previous agreement between the administrations concerned and those having services operating in accordance with the table of frequency allocations, which may be affected.[45]

Coverage Area

The coverage area is determined by the size of the country or
countries requiring particular service and it is the ideal function of
the satellite antenna to concentrate the radiation in the intended coverage area. Current techniques of antenna design allow carefully shaped
radiation patterns (beam shaping) which minimize spillover into adjacent
countries. Article VII (section 428A) of the radio regulations adopted by
the ITU provides that in arranging the technical characteristics of a
broadcasting satellite service a country is obliged to take all technical
means available to reduce to a maximum extent practical the radiation
over the territory of other countries unless an agreement has been previously reached with such countries.[46] Furthermore, provisional procedures for technical coordination between stations in the broadcasting
satellite service and other space systems and for coordination between
stations in the broadcasting satellite service and terrestrial radial systems (cable, networks) have been adopted by the ITU.

Reception Quality

Reception quality is inter alia a function of satellite power and
it can be shown that while good quality can be achieved over the entire service area, there is a strong economic relationship between the
two factors. Generally that reception quality would be at least equal
to that achieved with terrestrial systems.

Receiving Equipment

Depending on the choice of transmission method (frequency band,
modulation method, quality objectives, and so on), it is necessary to
envisage the need for converters to adapt existing receivers or for entirely new types of receivers. Different antennas must also be considered. It may be of interest to note that for particular applications
or requirements, substantial reductions in satellite transmitting power,
launching requirements, and related costs may be achieved by utilizing
more elaborate receiving equipment which would provide for community
receiving arrangements. Typical cost figures for providing converters
to existing domestic receivers vary according to complexity, sensitivity,
and numbers produced.

The Regulation of Spectrum and Orbit

Communication by satellite depends upon the use of a portion
of the radio frequency spectrum. The prospect of a number of separate
systems engaged in satellite broadcasting therefore raises the question

of whether existing frequency allocations, and others that might be made in desirable portions of the spectrum will be adequate to accommodate the likely demand.[47] The availability of frequencies is not the only variable in the equation, however. Both sending and receiving earth stations are designed with their antennas pointed at the satellite in their own system. If that satellite is spaced sufficiently far from any other satellite transmitting on the same frequencies, the systems can operate without harmful interference from the second satellite.[48] Presently available technology requires that the satellites must be spaced at least two degrees apart, so that on technical grounds 180 satellites is the absolute limit of the capacity of the geostationary satellite orbit.[49]

The limitations of satellite positions raise difficult legal problems that were tackled at the World Administrative Radio Conference for Space Telecommunications in 1971. The most important feature of the provisions adopted at this conference was that the status, guaranteeing the international protection of duly recorded frequency assignments which was applied to the terrestrial services, was not granted to stations in the space service. The resolutions admitted by the WARC (space) constitute an attempt to preclude any monopoly of frequency assignments suitable for use by the space radio communication services. It was decided that these assignments should not provide any permanent priority for any individual country or groups of countries and should not create an obstacle to the establishment of space systems by other countries.[50]

This new regulatory approach was based on the following considerations. The recognition of priority rights in the case of terrestrial stations was regarded as both normal and natural from the standpoint of international law since every state is technically and economically able to operate nonspace radio communication services on a footing of equality. With space communications, however, the situation was different since the ability to launch and operate artificial space objects is confined—at least for the present and the near future—to the handful of countries which possess the necessary technical and economic potential. "The recognition of any priority rights of these countries would constitute an obstacle to the subsequent establishment of space systems by other states."[51]

At its New Delhi Conference in 1974, the International Law Association discussed the validity of the so-called first-come-first-served principle with regard to the stationing of geostationary satellites in outer space. Some participants expressed the view that the principle was still adequate because up to 180 satellites may be placed in geostationary satellite orbit and "it will be quite a long time before this number is actually exhausted."[52] The West German participants contended that the principle of equal use offers only an "equal legal chance to each state of being the first one to use this or that orbital parking space."[53] Aldo A. Cocca (Argentina) and Marco Marcoff (Switzerland)

took the opposite view. Cocca was of the opinion that the principle
of first-come-first-served lacked a juridical basis in space law:

> The spectrum and the geo-stationary orbit are limited
> natural resources which form part of the common heritage
> of mankind. The access of all States, without any kind
> of discrimination, must be ensured, and all States . . .
> must co-operate . . . to facilitate the access of those
> countries which have not yet completed their develop-
> ment.[54]

Marcoff contended that this principle was inadequate in matters of
outer space activities: "It is a sequence of the 'classic' terrestrial
law of occupation of territories. Unilateral stationing of satellites
in geo-stationary orbits is in fact a disguised form of . . . appropriation, because such an activity excludes all others from doing so."[55]

At the ITU conference held in Torremolinos in September-October
1973, a decision was taken to hold late in 1976 or early in 1977 a
Planning Conference on Broadcasting by Satellite.[56] It was hoped that
this conference will alleviate some of the above problems through co-
operative international efforts and prior planning.

Objectives and Patterns of Use

Direct satellite broadcasting represents a new activity combining
features from at least four different areas: space technology, radio
communication, broadcasting, and information activities. While hitherto
these four areas have been governed by concepts and rules created in-
dependently of and not necessarily in concordance with each other,
a Swedish-Canadian working paper observed, the very fact of combination has added a new dimension which makes a planned coordinated,
cross-disciplinary approach to satellite broadcasting essential.[57]

The Working Group on Direct Broadcast Satellites at its second
session in 1969, mentioned among the objectives of satellite broadcasting the advancement of the principles and purposes of the United
Nations; the increase of knowledge, by the peoples of all countries,
of current events in the world, and of each other's cultures, beliefs,
and social interests; improved education and health benefits; greater
flow of news and information of general interest; and cultural programs
and the development of closer ties between peoples, within and between countries. Specifically, direct broadcasting from satellites into
community receivers will permit the acceleration of programs of national
integration, and economic and social development in such areas as
agriculture, health and family planning, community development, and
culture.[58]

According to its mandate, UNESCO has formulated a number of positive objectives to be achieved by satellite communication. These include the expansion of the free flow of information, education, the universal dissemination of knowledge, cultural exchange, and economic, social, and cultural development. All these objectives are to be met on the basis of and with a view to fruitful international cooperation. For example, satellite-borne television for educational purposes could serve in campaigns against illiteracy, in securing universal primary education and extending secondary and higher education, in raising the efficiency of present educational systems, in introducing new subject matter and new methodology, and in equalizing educational opportunities. With particular reference to developing countries, UNESCO has stated:

> Satellite broadcasting thus makes nation-wide television possible much sooner than by conventional means. Taken in conjunction with new techniques of tele-education, space communication would enable developing countries to accelerate the educational process. . . . Furthermore, satellite communication can reinforce links between communities and thus help to strengthen the bonds of national identity and contribute to nation-building.[59]

There are three main geographical patterns of use: national, regional, and global. There is a very limited number of countries large enough to warrant domestic use of broadcast satellites. Geographically smaller countries would most likely have to form a "region" for satellite broadcasting purposes as has been suggested for South America or Western Europe. Such domestic systems, although they would require international cooperation to ensure frequency and orbital coordination, would not raise any new international problems.

As is the case of present satellite communication systems, it is possible to imagine satellite broadcasting systems with a view to global coverage. However, owing to difficulties raised by differences in technical standards, time zones, varying program interest and viewing patterns, and economic considerations, such systems are not likely to be established. Judging from present experience, the wide or global distribution of programs will remain a rare occurrence, limited to the coverage of very special events such as the Olympic Games and coronations.

In view of the small number of countries likely to establish domestic systems and the improbability of global systems it would appear that the most practical and probable pattern of use will be the regional.[60] This designation refers to the use of satellite broadcasting according to agreements between countries of the same geographical area. The regional concept is based upon the idea of participation of all the countries and organizational problems.

While recognizing the different structures and roles of broadcasting in different countries, the UN working group called attention to
the existing regional cooperation between broadcasters with regard to
procedures concerning program content in regional or international
broadcast transmissions as a basis for arrangements concerning broadcasting from satellites. Its second report noted the many-faceted co-
operation between broadcasters grouped in such regional associations
as the Asian Broadcasting Union (ABU), the European Broadcasting
Union (EBU), the International Organization of Radio and Television
(OIRT), and the Union des Radiodiffusions et Televisions Nationales
Africaines (URTNA).[61] Also, at the UNESCO meeting of governmental
experts in December 1969, there was agreement that much could be
learned from the experience and present practices of these broadcasting
unions.[62]

Planned Systems of Direct
Satellite Broadcasting

According to the previously mentioned UN working group time-
table for the technical feasibility of the various sytems of direct
satellite broadcasting, all current efforts are directed to the establishment of a system which provides for reception by community receivers.[63] Plans for experiments in the use of direct broadcast satellites or for establishment of such satellite systems have advanced
in many parts of the world. The first experiments in the use of this
technology have taken place in the United States. As part of a Department of Health, Education, and Welfare (HEW) experiment, the ATS-6
satellite, which was launched in 1974, has been used to broadcast
educational material, to augment existing classroom courses, directly
into junior high schools located in remote areas of the Rocky Mountains.
In another part of the HEW experiment, the ATS-6 satellite system has
been used to bring university courses at the graduate level to practicing
teachers in the Appalachia area. In yet another aspect of the experiment, the ATS-6 satellite has been used by the Veterans Administration
for medical education and consultation, and in Alaska experiments
were conducted to develop the information needed to meet the state's
specific telecommunications requirements with respect to education,
health, cultural exchange, entertainment, and interconnection facilities
to provide live programming to the general population.[64]

After completion of the experiments in the United States, the
ATS-6 satellite was moved by the end of May 1975 to a position over
the Indian Ocean. In accordance with the agreement concluded in 1969
between the Indian Department of Atomic Energy and the U.S. National
Aeronautics and Space Administration (NASA), the satellite will be used
for the Satellite Instructional Television Experiment (SITE) for about a

year. SITE will broadcast programs to about 5,000 selected villages
of which about 3,000 will receive the signal for rebroadcasting by
regular television transmitters, and about 2,000 for direct viewing on
community receivers.[65] The Indian authorities alone will be responsible
for the earth segment and programming. The primary instructional objectives are to contribute to family planning programs, to improve ag-
ricultural practices, and to contribute to national integration. The
secondary instructional objectives include in-school and adult education, and teacher and vocational training.[66]

The Brazilian educational satellite program, known under the title
Satellite Avancado de Comunicaciones Interdisciplinares (SACI), is
designed to apply the systems approach to the possible use of a geostationary satellite to improve the capability of the educational system
and to provide a number of communication services. In the first phase
which started in January 1972, experiments have been carried out between the Instituto Nacional de Pesquisas Espacias (INPE), in Sao Jose
dos Compos, and the University of Stanford. During the second phase,
the intention will be to demonstrate the advantages of communications
systems based on both terrestrial and space techniques. A comprehensive educational experiment will be undertaken in Rio Grande del Norte.
For the actual satellite experiment, INPE has submitted a proposal to
NASA for the use of ATS-6; it is presently under study. The third phase
envisages the use of a Brazilian-owned satellite for education and communications services.[67]

In April 1971, the Canadian Department of Communications, in
cooperation with NASA, established an experimental project entitled
Communications Technology Satellite (CTS). The objective of CTS,
which was to be launched in 1975, is to investigate the operation of
a high-power satellite to provide two-way voice communications, FM
broadcast, and data transmission and color TV broadcasts for communities with low-cost ground terminals. Particular emphasis will be placed
on communication to remote areas in Canada. The use of high-power
traveling wave tubes (TWTs) in the satellite, operating in the 12 Giga-
hertz (GHz) band, will enable the cost and size of ground terminals
to be minimized.[68]

Following a number of preliminary investigations, a feasibility
study by the United Nations Development Program (UNDP) has been
conducted in South America on a regional satellite system for education,
culture, and development information. The countries cooperating in
this study were Argentina, Bolivia, Chile, Colombia, Ecuador, Para-
guay, Peru, Uruguay, and Venezuela. The basic concept envisions a
regional organization established by the Spanish-speaking countries
in the area, which would be responsible for the development and operation of a regional system which would use various communication
media, including broadcast satellites, to distribute educational and
cultural programs to approximately 20 million students of all grades
and about 15 million adults in 150,000 community reception centers
connected to some 600,000 television receivers.[69]

Preliminary investigations have been undertaken in the Arab region, at the request of governments in the area, by regional organizations (the League of Arab States, the Arab States Broadcasting Union) as well as by international organizations (UNESCO/ITU). The results of these studies have tended to confirm the potential advantages of satellite communications among Arab countries, and for the transmission of television programs for community reception in order to meet the educational and information requirements of individual countries or groups of countries.[70]

Further studies of the use of broadcast satellite services for educational purposes have also been undertaken in Indonesia, Africa (south of the Sahara), and Southeast Asia, and for both educational and general programming in Western Europe, both on a national and regional level.[71]

It is clear from the above review of current experimentation with DBS that the type of broadcasting satellite configurations which are being envisaged for the foreseeable future would be largely domestic systems, established by a state to provide service over its own territory, with no intent to serve any other country; and regional systems, established by a group of countries to serve the territory of the region which they jointly constitute. There are no plans for more ambitious community reception systems providing full global coverage.

NOTES

1. Wireless World, October 1945, quoted in Edward W. Ploman, Kommunikation durch Satelliten (Mainz: v. Hase & Koehler, 1974), p. 35.

2. Edward W. Ploman, A Guide to Satellite Communication (Paris: UNESCO, 1972), p. 8 (hereafter cited as Guide). This booklet appeared in the UNESCO series, Report and Papers on Mass Communications, and continues to be the best introduction to the wide range of issues surrounding satellite communication. The author has largely relied on it in this section.

3. Guide. See also L. Jaffe, "Technical Possibilities for Radio and Television Services by Satellites," in UNESCO, Communication in the Space Age (Paris: UNESCO, 1968), pp. 131-37.

4. Guide, p. 9.

5. Ibid.

6. Ibid.

7. Ibid.

8. S. Houston Lay and Howard J. Taubenfeld, The Law Relating to Activities of Man in Space (Chicago: University of Chicago Press, 1970), pp. 110-11.

9. Ibid., p. 111.

10. Ibid.

11. Guide, p. 9.

12. Ibid.

13. Ibid., p. 12.

14. Ibid.

15. Lay and Taubenfeld, op. cit., p. 115. For an elaboration on the relationship between East and West on this matter, see I. Mc-Daniel and L. Day, "INTELSAT and Communist Nations' Policy on Communications Satellites," Journal of Broadcasting 18, no. 3 (Summer 1974): pp. 311-21.

16. Guide, p. 14.

17. U.S. Communications Satellite Corporation (COMSAT), Annual Report to the President and The Congress, Washington, D.C., 1974 p. 17 (hereafter cited as Annual Report). See also International Telecommunications Satellite Organization (INTELSAT) 1974-75 INTEL-SAT Annual Report, Washington, D.C., and for most current figures, a recent INTELSAT Press Release, February 13 1976, 76-7-M, p. 2.

18. Annual Report, p. 18, and INTELSAT Press Release, 76-7-M, p. 2. See also A. W. Frutkin, "Space Communications and the Developing Countries," in Communications Technology and Social Policy (New York: John Wiley & Sons, 1973), pp. 369-74.

19. Annual Report, p. 35.

20. Ibid., p. 122. For foreign policy implications of Satellite Communications see Sig Mickelson, "Communications by Satellite," Foreign Affairs 48 (October 1969): pp. 67-79.

21. Lay and Taubenfeld, op. cit., p. 120.

22. Ibid.

23. Ibid.

24. Ibid., p. 122.

25. Quoted in ibid.

26. Guide, p. 14. For technical details see N. I. Tchistiakov, "Evolution of Satellites and Orbits," in Communications in the Space Age (Paris: UNESCO, 1968), pp. 138-46.

27. I. Petrov. "Intersputnik: International Space Communication System and Organization," Telecommunication Journal 39 (November 1972): p. 679.

28. Ibid., p. 680.

29. "Intersputnik," Unitar News 5, no. 2 (1973): p. 8.

30. Ibid.

31. Abram Chayes et al., Satellite Broadcasting (London: Oxford University Press, 1971), pp. 2-3.

32. Ibid., p. 3.

33. Ibid.

34. Ibid.

35. Addendum to the Report of the Outer Space Committee, UN Document A/7621/Add. 1 (1969) pp. 10-11.

36. Cited in Chayes et al., op. cit., p. 4.

37. Model 84AP-Spa2 in International Telecommunication Union, Final Acts (of the World Administrative Radio Conference for Space Telecommunications), Geneva, 1971, p. 41 (hereafter cited as Final Acts).

38. Ibid., p. 42.

39. Ibid.

40. In this section the author has relied largely on the survey of the technical and economic considerations of direct television broadcasting from satellite, reproduced as Annex VI in UN Document A/AC.105/127 (1974).

41. Guide, p. 9.

42. Final Acts, pp. 312-20.

43. Ibid.

44. Ibid.

45. Ibid., pp. 155-82.

46. Ibid., p. 117.

47. Chayes et al., op. cit., p. 15.

48. Ibid.

49. International Law Association, New Delhi Conference, (pamphlet), 1974, p. 5 (hereafter cited as New Delhi Conference).

50. Ibid., p. 12.

51. Ibid.

52. Ibid., p. 42.

53. Ibid., p. 43.

54. Ibid., p. 41.

55. Ibid., p. 42.

56. Felix Fernandez-Shaw, "The New International Telecommunication Convention of Malaga-Torremolinos (1973)," E.B.U. Review 25, no. 2 (March 1974), p. 26.

57. UN Document A/AC.105/WG.3/L.1 (1970), p. 11. For more details see a working paper presented by Canada and Sweden to the Working Group on Direct Broadcast Satellites (DBS), upon which the author has partly relied in this section. UN Document A/AC.105/WG.3/L1 (1970).

58. UN Document A/AC.105/66 (1969).

59. UNESCO, Final Report (Meeting of Governmental Experts on International Arrangements in the Space Communication Field, December 2-9, 1969), UNESCO Document COM/MD15, p. 7 (hereafter cited as Final Report).

60. UN Document A/AC.105/66 (1969), and UN Document A/AC.105/WG.3/L.1 (1970), pp. 15-16. For the same view see Paul L. Laskin and Abram Chayes, "A Brief History of the Issues," in Values in Conflict, p. 6.

61. UN Document A/7261/Add.1, p. 38; cited in UN Document A/AC.105/WG.3/L.1 (1970), pp. 25-26.

62. Final Report; cited in UN Document A/AC.105/WG.3/L.1 (1970), p. 26.

63. For more detailed information see the reports of the Working Group on DBS, 1969-74. This overview which considers systems that have reached a concrete planning stage prior to 1974 draws, among other sources, on a Canadian-Swedish working paper of 1973 (A/AC. 105/WG.3/L.4). For current developments see the trade press (for example, Aviation Week and Space Technology) and Peter B. White's most useful Satellite, Telecommunications and Education: A Calendar of Future Events (Syracuse: Syracuse University Research Corporation, 1975).

64. James J. Gehring, "Broadcasting Satellites—Prospects and Problems" (Paper presented at the 17th Colloquium on the Law of Outer Space, International Institute of Space Law, Amsterdam, September 30-October 5, 1974), pp. 16-17.

65. UN Document A/AC.105/WG.3/L.4 (1973), p. 5. For more information about the SITE project see UN Document A/AC.105/114 (1972); Chayes et al., op. cit., pp. 13-15; and Guide, p. 20.

66. UN Document A/AC.105/WG.3/L.4 (1973), p. 5. See also Kenneth A. Polcyn, An Educator's Guide to Communication Satellite Technology (Washington, D.C.: Academy for Educational Development, 1973), pp. 64-68.

67. UN Document A/AC.105/WG.3/L.4 (1973), p. 5; Polcyn, op. cit., pp. 69-76.

68. UN Document A/AC.105/WG.3/L.4 (1973), p. 6.

69. Ibid. See also A. H. Ghani, "Looking Forward to the Second Fifteen Years in Space," Unitar News 5, no. 2 (1973), pp. 4-5.

70. UN Document A/AC.105/WG.3/L.4 (1973), p. 6. See also report of UNESCO to the Working Group on DBS, UN Document A/AC. 105/WG.3/L.5 (1973).

71. Ibid.

2

THE EMERGING LAW
OF SPACE COMMUNICATIONS

The purpose of this chapter is to describe the development since the early 1960s of the basic principles of the new international law of space communication which emerged in the larger context of the law of outer space. As such these principles are relevant to direct satellite broadcasting.

Space law is that body of international legal norms which has been developed since the beginning of the 1960s, primarily under the auspices of the United Nations General Assembly and its Committee on the Peaceful Uses of Outer Space which was established by the General Assembly in 1958[1] and reconstituted as a permanent committee in 1959.[2] Three seminal General Assembly resolutions in the period 1961-63 laid the groundwork for what came to be known as the law of space communication.

On December 20, 1961, General Assembly Resolution 1721 passed unanimously, providing that outer space should be used only for mankind's betterment and for the benefit of all states regardless of the level of their economic or scientific development. The following year, on December 19, 1962, the General Assembly adopted unanimously its Resolution 1802, which invited UN agencies "to give sympathetic consideration to requests from Member States for technical and financial assistance to supplement their own resources for these activities." The General Assembly

> Believes that communication by satellite offers great
> benefits to mankind as it will permit the expansion of
> radio, telephone and television transmissions, including
> the broadcast of United Nations activities, thus facilitat-
> ing contact among the peoples of the world.[3]

On December 13, 1963, Resolution 1962, a Declaration of Legal Principles Governing the Activities of States in the Exploration and Use of Outer Space, was unanimously passed, to become, in the

21

words of one author, the "twelve tables" of space law.[4] Most of these
principles were thereafter incorporated in the Treaty of Principles Governing the Activities of States in the Exploration and Use of Outer Space,
Including the Moon and Other Celestial Bodies."[5] The treaty received
the unanimous commendation of the assembly in Resolution 2222 of
December 19, 1966. It was opened for signature by all states on January 27, 1967, simultaneously at London, Moscow, and Washington,
and came into force in October 1967, having by then been signed by
ninety-three states and ratified by sixteen, including the three depos-
itory states.[6]

FRAMEWORK FOR REGULATION

The principles embodied in both the declaration and the treaty
constitute a framework for the international regulation of all space
activities and are therefore applicable also to satellite broadcasting.[7]
In the view of the author of the basic UNESCO Guide to Satellite Communication, the formulation of legislative provisions for space has
been approached intellectually "in a fashion very different from traditional notions of international law."[8] Through the process of evolution from recommendatory motions to treaty law,[9] five basic principles
have been developed which constitute cornerstones of the legal framework regulating man's activities in outer space: free use, sovereign
equality of states, prohibition of national appropriation, state responsibility, common interest of all mankind.

The Principles of Free Use and
Sovereign Equality of States

Article I (2) of the Space Treaty states: "Outer space . . . shall
be free for exploration and use by all states without discrimination of
any kind, on a basis of equality . . . and there shall be free access.
. . . " This article constitutes at one time an elaborate and vague
compromise between these two principles that, as Gotlieb and Dalfen
observed, "may in fact collide or tend in different directions."[10] Thus
"free use" to one country "might be a wide-ranging expansive term with
respect both to potential uses and users, encompassing free enterprise
in space, and so forth. Others might take a more restricted view.
. . ."[11] Similarly, sovereign equality "might be regarded as one of
equal rights of access to space exploration systems, or alternatively,
to one of the equal rights to the economic resources and technological
means to set up one's own system."[12] Erik N. Valters observed the
same tendency in Article I. It represents both an endorsement of the

idea that there should be no monopoly of space communications by any
single state or group of states and of a laissez faire approach to international space communications, since every state, in principle, is
left free to launch as many satellites as it desires.[13]

As a result, the principle of the freedom to use outer space is
frequently invoked as an argument by states which are unwilling to subject their present or future space communications activities to international limitation or regulation. At the same time the notions of equality and nondiscrimination are used to support the view that all states
should not only have access to a global communications satellite system, but also that they should be able to particpate in the formulation
of the policies of the system on an equalitarian and nondiscriminatory
basis. Similarly, it was argued that the concepts of equality and
nondiscrimination make it unlawful for the space powers to grant pref-
erential treatment to selected nonspace powers, and that therefore a
bilateral cooperative arrangement such as the Indian-American SITE project should be available, in principle, to all developing countries regardless of the state of their relations to the space power concerned.[14]

The Principle of Prohibition of National Appropriation

Article II of the space treaty states: "Outer space . . . is not
subject to national appropriation by claim of sovereignty, by means of
use or occupation, or by any other means." Applied to satellite broadcasting, this principle raises the previously mentioned controversy
(see Chapter 1) as to whether a state can legally claim a particular
orbital "parking slot" on the basis of the first-come-first-served principle. However, the decisions taken by the World Administrative
Radio Conference for Space Telecommunications in 1971, that frequency
assignments for space communication should not provide any permanent
priority for any individual country, together with the 1977 Planning Conference on Broadcasting by Satellite should settle a good deal of these
issues.

The Principle of State Responsibility

It has been explicitly set out in Article VI of the treaty that
"states shall bear international responsibility for activities in outer
space . . . whether such activities are carried on by government
agencies or by non-governmental entities. . . ." This principle is
the result of a compromise between two different concepts of economic
and social organization. Originally the United States and other Western

countries maintained that "private and semi-private bodies might undertake space activities in the future," while the Soviet Union suggested a rule to the effect that "activities pertaining to the exploration and use of outer space should be carried out exclusively by States."[15]

Finally, there is the principle of common interest of all mankind that is set forth in the treaty in Article I (1): "The exploration and use of outer space . . . shall be carried out for the benefit and in the interest of all countries, irrespective of their degree of economic or scientific development, and shall be the province of all mankind." This language gave rise to many discussions as to whether mankind has become—or is in the process of becoming—a subject of international law in addition to the traditional ones, such as states, international organizations, individuals.[16]

Although the interpretation of the above principles is not universally agreed upon, and despite their vagueness, they form a sound basis—not to a small extent because of the overwhelming political support the space treaty received—for the discussion of the ordering of the direct broadcast satellite.

NOTES

1. General Assembly Resolution 1348 (XIII), December 13, 1958. For a description of the early history of the committee see L. Meeker, "The First Decade of the Law in Space," International Lawyer 3 (January 1969): pp. 195-6.

2. General Assembly Resolutions 1348 (XIII), December 13, 1958, and 1472 (XIV), December 12, 1959.

3. Quoted by Eilene Galloway, in "Broadcast Satellites," (paper presented at Seventh Colloquium on the Law of Outer Space, International Institute of Space Law, Amsterdam, Netherlands, September 30-October 5, 1974).

4. C. W. Jenks, "Space Law Becomes a Reality," Current Problems in Space Law: A Symposium 15 (London, 1966); quoted in "Case Study," p. 35.

5. For text of space treaty see General Assembly Resolution 2222 (XXI), Annex A, December 19, 1966.

6. "Case Study," p. 35.

7. Guide, p. 26.

8. Ibid.

9. "Case Study," p. 35.

10. Ibid. For further interpretation see Stephen Gorove, "Freedom of Exploration and Use in the Outer Space Treaty," Denver Journal of International Law and Policy 1 (Fall 1971), pp. 93-107.

11. "Case Study," p. 35.

12. Ibid.

13. Erik N. Valters, "International Law of Communications Satellites: Scarce Resources in a New Environment" (Ph.D. diss., Columbia University, 1970), p. 148.

14. Ibid., pp. 149-50.

15. UN Documents A/C.1/SR.1296 (1962) and A/5181 (1962), Annex III; both quoted in Valters, op. cit., pp. 161-62.

16. For a discussion of this issue see, for example: Ernst Fasan, "The Meaning of the Term 'Mankind' in Space Legal Language," Journal of Space Law 2, no. 2 (1974): pp. 125-31; Ulrich Thieme, Rundfunk-satelliten und Internationales Recht (Hamburg: Hansischer Gildenver-lag, 1973).

3

**DIRECT BROADCAST
SATELLITES AND THE
UNITED NATIONS**

THE EMERGENCE OF THE ISSUE:
1963-68

The purpose of the following section is to describe and document the events and diplomatic moves that ultimately led to the establishment of the UN Working Group on Direct Broadcast Satellites within the Committee on the Peaceful Uses of Outer Space in 1968.[1] In
less than six years since the question of direct broadcast satellites
(DBS) was first (indirectly) touched upon in the committee, "a first
plateau in the gradual evolution of international legal norms governing the activity had been reached."[2] It will be shown how the issue
has steadily gained momentum, due partly to ongoing technological
progress, partly to subtle shifts in the overall distribution of power
and influence within the UN system. Also, the information gained from
this overview should facilitate the analysis of the period 1969-75 and
place it in historical perspective.

In November 1963, Brazil indirectly raised the problems relating
to DBS in the Outer Space Committee when it was discussing the draft
declaration of legal principles: "The declaration should also incor-
porate a ban on the utilization of a communication system based on
satellites for purposes of encouraging national, racial or class rival-
ries and a reference to some international scrutiny of global satellite
communication."[3] The declaration which was adopted by the General
Assembly in December 1963 sought to cover the Brazilian position by
including in its preamble a reference to the assembly's Resolution 110
of November 3, 1947, which condemned "propaganda designed or likely
to provoke or encourage any threat to the peace, breach of peace, or
act of aggression." This 1947 resolution was considered applicable
to outer space.[4]

The issue of DBS was for the first time raised directly in 1964.
A working paper prepared by the UN Secretariat for the Scientific and

Technical Subcommittee of the Outer Space Committee pointed out that
a viable program in the field of space communication should look to the
future "when the possibility of direct broadcast satellites able to transmit programs direct to the receiving radio or television sets of ordinary
listeners and viewers at their homes becomes feasible."[5] Experts were
quoted as predicting that this development was likely to take place
within the next ten years. The paper, then, suggested the following
course of action. As a first step, a panel of experts should prepare
studies of selected aspects of the problem. Their work, while essentially scientific and technical, should also provide the necessary basic
information to permit subsequent consideration at a more general level.
The panel of experts, therefore, should be drawn from a number of relevant fields, that is, telecommunications, information media, economics,
and sociology, and perhaps political science and international law.
Upon the basis of such detailed, accurate, and specific studies, a
seminar of carefully selected participants should be organized "in,
say, 1966,"[6] in order to bring about a systematic investigation of the
political, social, legal, and economic implications of DBS at an international level. All this should provide a sound basis for further specific recommendations, to "make space communications an effective
instrument of international co-operation."[7]

     The early interest of the Soviet Union in questions surrounding
direct satellite broadcasting became apparent from its proposal "that
the outer space committee consider the questions relating to the use
of satellites for transmitting radio and television programs intended
for direct reception by the general public after the report of the International Radio Consultive Committee (CCIR) on this subject has been
received by ITU."[8] This proposal was adopted by the scientific and
technical subcommittee.[9]

     In 1965, in the Outer Space Committee Working Group to Organize
the UN Conference on Outer Space, the Brazilian delegate proposed that
the agenda of the conference should include the discussion of questions
relating to DBS, especially to "the question of the cultural and political
impact of television programs transmitted by artificial satellites."[10]
This matter was not, however, included in the agenda of the conference,
but left for further and more detailed study.[11]

     The Legal Subcommittee of the Outer Space Committee met in 1966
to discuss the draft treaty on outer space. During this session, various
references were made to direct satellite broadcasting. Introducing the
seventh preambular paragraph which mentioned General Assembly Resolution 110 of 1947 and made it applicable to outer space, the Soviet
delegate also referred to DBS: "It will soon be possible for conventional television sets to receive broadcasts direct from satellites. Hence
legal measures were urgently needed to prevent a great technical achiev-
ment from being used against the interests of peace."[12] Commenting
on the draft, the Brazilian delegate saw the need for "some kind of
international scrutiny of the use of outer space for the purpose of

telecommunications and the transmission of television programs,"[13] and on July 26, 1966, the United Arab Republic (UAR) submitted a working paper proposing a new article for the draft treaty:

> The parties to the treaty, recognizing the enormous
> potentialities of space applications for sound and tele-
> vision broadcasting, undertake to make use of such ap-
> plications only in accordance with the resolutions of the
> General Assembly which condemn using the media of in-
> formation for hostile propaganda, and urge states to uti-
> lize them for promoting friendly relations among nations,
> based upon the purposes and principles of the charter.
> In particular, they shall undertake to regulate at the
> world-wide level, direct broadcasting by artificial
> satellites, as regards both its technical and program
> contents aspects. They undertake to refrain from using
> communication satellites for direct broadcasting until
> such regulations are set by the competent international
> organizations.[14]

The reaction to this UAR proposal by the committee members was indicative of the differing opinions and attitudes as well as national interests that were to shape numerous future discussions on DBS. The delegations of the Soviet Union, Brazil, India, Czechoslovakia, France, and Mexico[15] warmly received the proposal or at least associated themselves with the underlying thought of this new article, while the United States and the United Kingdom[16] stressed the need for further study. They raised the question of whether worldwide regulation of program content was not in conflict with domestic communications systems in various countries.

Despite the widespread sympathy that the UAR-proposed article received, it was nevertheless recognized that far more research and discussion was necessary, and that it was premature to insert the article in the treaty before the question had been more fully investigated.[17] The Outer Space Treaty adopted on December 19, 1966, then, sought to deal with the matter by starting in preambular paragraph 8 as follows:

> Taking account of United Nations General Assembly
> Resolution 110 (II) of November 3, 1947, which condemned
> propaganda designed or likely to provoke or encourage
> any threat to the peace, breach of the peace or act of
> aggression, and considering that the aforementioned
> resolution is applicable to outer space.[18]

In the First Committee (which is part of the General Assembly) on December 17, 1966, the UAR, Mexico, and Chile proposed that

the study of the utilization of outer space should include the study of
space communications[19] and on December 19, 1966, the General Assembly adopted a resolution which requested the Outer Space Committee "to begin the study of questions relative to the definition of outer
space and the utilization of outer space and celestial bodies including
the various implications of space communications."[20]

In April 1967, the Outer Space Committee considered the organization of its work and in relation to this mandate. The French delegate, echoing a certain amount of concern with regard to future DBS
activities of numerous countries, suggested that the study should include the question of the possibility of regulation in this matter. He
contended that the regulations of the ITU did not, in fact, seem adequate at the time to protect states against the risk of any "saturation
broadcasting"[21] by any other state.[22] The delegations of the UAR and
the USSR supported this proposal while the U.S. delegate spoke in
favor of a study at the technical level in the scientific and technical
subcommittee contending that at the outset a great deal of technical
clarification seems to be necessary.[23]

In 1967, during the discussions in the legal subcommittee on
the agenda item space communications, a statement by the Czechoslovak delegate alluded for the first time to what the content of future
regulation of DBS might be:

> Those principles should include, as indicated in the
> Treaty of January 1967, the principle that all States had
> the right to use outer space for space communications
> and bore responsibility for any such activities, and, in
> addition, the principles that satellite broadcasting and
> transmission must serve the interests of international
> peace and security and must respect the sovereign
> equality of all States.[24]

The significant role later to be played by Sweden—in cooperation
with Canada—became apparent during the discussions in the First Committee in 1967. Sweden's delegate clearly took sides in the previously
mentioned conflict between the legislative and operational approach
to DBS: "I do not wish to dramatize the situation unduly, but believe
it is safe to say that if we are to avoid chaos it will be necessary,
before technical developments have reached the stage when such
satellites are put into operation, to establish some rules governing
their utilization."[25] Therefore, he added, the question of DBS should
be placed on the agenda of the Committee on Outer Space as one requiring careful study in all aspects.[26] Czechoslovakia reiterated its
position and stressed the concept of national sovereignty of states.
The UAR delegate emphasized the need for regulation of program content[27] and France expressed its disappointment with the slow progress
of the committee work on this matter.[28]

A big step forward was the General Assembly Resolution of the same year in which paragraph 13 specifically requested the Outer Space Committee to study the question of DBS as follows:

> The Committee on the Peaceful Uses of Outer Space
> to study the technical feasibility of communications by
> direct broadcasts from satellites and the current and
> foreseeable developments in this field, as well as the
> implications of such developments.[29]

In 1968, during the consideration of the subject in the legal sub-committee, the Swedish delegate introduced a proposal requesting[30] that the question of direct broadcasting satellites be placed on the agenda of the scientific and technical subcommittee. His delegation felt that the legal subcommittee could not consider the legal aspects of the problem until it had received the proposed study by the scientific and technical subcommittee.[31] Following the Swedish proposal, the legal subcommittee adopted the following resolution on June 28, 1968:

> The Legal Sub-Committee on the Peaceful Uses of
> Outer Space,
> Having in mind paragraph 13 of General Assembly
> Resolution 2260 (XXII), entitled "Report of the Commit-
> tee on the Peaceful Uses of Outer Space,"
> Conscious of the importance and urgency of the prob-
> lem of the potentialities of the operation of direct broad-
> casting satellites,
> Recommend to the Committee on the Peaceful Uses of
> Outer Space that it request the Scientific and Technical
> Sub-Committee to consider the question of direct broad-
> casting satellites, with a view to preparing a study of
> the technical problems involved, enlisting whenever
> appropriate the assistance of the competent specialized
> agencies of the United Nations.[32]

At the Outer Space Committee meeting in October 1968 reference was made to the Vienna Conference on Outer Space of 1968 at which it had been suggested that satellites with very powerful transmitters could be produced within the next few years and direct television broadcast from satellites would be available in about five years. It was also remarked at the conference that such techniques were already in existence, but that the cost of establishing such a system at that time was one of the principal factors militating against it.[33] The Canadian delegate pointed out that "it could be decided in the very near future by any country or group of countries that the benefits to be derived from these new and untapped media outweigh the expens-es."[34]

With this new information available, a sense of urgency began
to spread within the committee. The recommendation of the legal sub-
committee of only four months previous (June 1968)[35] did not appear
to adequately take account of this new situation. A widespread feeling
that a study of the practical, legal, and social aspects, as well as
the technical aspects should be initiated as soon as possible, became
the basis for a proposal by the Swedish delegate. For the sake of ex-
pediting the matter, a special working group would be set up with the
mandate to undertake a study of all aspects of this particular problem.[36]
Among the concrete questions which would be studied by the proposal
were these:

> How to secure the right of States to avail themselves
> of satellite communications and how to promote organiza-
> tional and administrative arrangements to provide equit-
> able access to satellite systems for all States with special
> regard to smaller and to developing countries.
>   Furthermore, how to develop the use of satellite com-
> munications for different users, in particular, existing
> national broadcasting corporations, at the lowest possible
> prices.
>   How to promote efforts of the developing countries to
> use communication satellites in the field of education and
> economic and social development.
>   How to ensure equitable use of the radio-frequency
> spectrum.
>   How to promote the use of satellite communications
> in the public interest and for peaceful purposes.[37]

This proposal, which was jointly proposed by Sweden and Canada,
was favored by many other delegations[38] and, at the instigation of
these two countries, the Outer Space Committee recommended action.[39]
Its report, after noting General Assembly Resolution 2260, the legal
subcommittee's resolution of June 1968, and the "widespread interest"
in direct broadcasting at the UN Conference on the Peaceful Uses of
Outer Space,[40] went on as follows:

> The Committee, in the light of these developments,
> considers that a working group should be set up to study
> and to report to the Committee on the technical feasibility
> of communications by direct broadcast from satellites and
> the current and foreseeable developments in this field as
> well as the implications of such developments, including
> comparative user costs and other economic considerations,
> as well as social, cultural, legal and other questions.
>   The first task of the working group would be to formu-
> late a work schedule for its fields of study and establish

a time-table. It shall, early in 1969, address itself
to a study of the technical feasibility and technical
characteristics of direct broadcasting from satellites
including questions relating to user costs, informing
itself of and fully utilizing the work in this field done
by the ITU and other specialized agencies, and shall
prepare a report. On the basis of this report, the working group shall then proceed to consider additional
economic as well as social, cultural, legal and other
implications of direct broadcasting, again preparing
a report on these implications. Both reports of the
working group shall be transmitted to the Committee
to enable it to report on the matter to the General
Assembly, at its twenty-fourth session.[41]

The report suggested that the working group should be composed
of interested members of the Outer Space Committee, "represented in
so far as possible by specialists."[42] and that representatives of the
specialized agencies of the United Nations shall be invited to participate in the work of the group.[43]

SUMMARY

Various patterns of international conduct can be discerned on
the basis of the above discussion. Just as the manner in which an
issue is created and initially perceived can determine its further development, a preliminary analysis of the patterns of this issue's origin-
ation and early perception should be helpful in defining the basic lines
of evolution of DBS in the years 1969 through 1975. For the present
purposes, the isolation of three motivational patterns underlying political and diplomatic behavior with respect to DBS should illustrate
the overall trends of the period under investigation: the patterns of
fear (concern), urgency, and study.

The Pattern of Fear

The old truism that fear rather than hope spurs political action,
appears to apply fully to the issue of DBS. From the very beginning,
concerns about possible abuse of DBS in particular and space communications in general, were at the heart of the international debate.
Certainly, reference was made to DBS's positive potential with regard
to education and nation building and its great technical achievement
was praised; the main emphasis, however, rested with DBS as a source
of possible friction. Both the Socialist countries and the majority of
the developing nations tended toward this approach.

The Pattern of Urgency

Closely related to the pattern of fear, that of urgency stresses
the need for prompt action. Legal measures were urgently needed if
we were to avoid chaos. This sense of urgency cleared the way for
the legislative approach that favors regulation prior to experience.
(The dichotomy between legislative and operational approach will be
dealt with in Chapter 5.) Again, a certain measure of identity of interests has evolved between the Eastern European countries and the
Third World nations joined by some Western and nonaligned states
(France, Canada, Sweden).

The Pattern of Study

Suspicious of hasty action, the study approach preferred careful
and detailed study of all the elements—mainly technical and economic—
involved in DBS. This pattern coincides with the operational approach
that advocates that experience with new technology must precede its
regulation. This study pattern, although closest to the Western nations—especially the United States—has usually gained wide acceptance within the committees as a convenient compromise formula that
does not preclude anything.

As for the nature of this preparatory legislative process itself,
the venue oscillated between the various subcommittees, the parent
Outer Space Committee, and the UN General Assembly as a source of
guiding majority will to decide over the basic course of action (for
example, in the composition of the agenda of the committee meetings).
The UN Conference on the Peaceful Uses of Outer Space of 1968 proved
to be of crucial importance for the committee work and led directly to
the establishment of the Working Group on Direct Broadcast Satellites
by the close of the same year.

Prior to 1967, when the General Assembly for the first time officially requested the Outer Space Committee to take on the question
of DBS, the debate was rather unstructured and statements on DBS were
made usually in the context of discussions on outer space in general.
Considerations of its technical feasibility gave way gradually to discussions on regulatory aspects. The crucial shift from a predominately
technical to a more interdisciplinary approach took place in the wake
of the Vienna Outer Space Conference (1968). The enormous publicity
generated by reports on the prospect of direct television broadcasting
from satellites prompted the committee to expand the narrow technical
approach and open up the debate to wider circles. Not unlike domestic
legislative processes, outside uncontrollable forces such as a wave
of publicity, can take an issue away from the experts and specialists
and allow the politicians to move in.

At the political level of the general distribution of power within
the UN system, the treatment of DBS during 1963-68 illustrates the

first sign of new alignments with the Eastern bloc and the majority of
the developing countries in one camp and the major Western powers
in the other. Still more than half a decade away from the celebrated
new majority of 1974 and 1975, the issue of DBS was an early indicator
of new identities of interests. In this context, Brazil may serve as a
useful example. A close ally of the United States in many areas of
general foreign and domestic policy, its position on DBS is hardly dis-
tinguishable from that of the Soviet Union: both urged control and
legislation of DBS.

Also, the compromise position of Canada and Sweden, that was
to have a great impact on the course of future discussion, already began to take shape. Associating itself with widely accepted elements
of thought of both camps, this position emerged as a rallying point
for the uncommitted.

THE WORKING GROUP ON
DIRECT BROADCAST SATELLITES:
1969–70

The First Meeting: February 1969

The Working Group on Direct Broadcast Satellites established to
study and report on the technical feasibility of communication by direct broadcast from satellites and on the current and foreseeable developments in this field, held its first series of eight meetings at UN
headquarters, in New York, between February 11 and February 20, 1969.
Olof Rydbeck of Sweden, at the time director general of Sveriges Radio
(Sweden), was elected chairman.

Of the 28 member states of the parent committee (the Committee
on the Peaceful Uses of Outer Space), 22 states were represented at
the meetings. The average delegation consisted of 2.8 representatives
and advisors. A few countries such as Canada, Italy, the United
States, and the Soviet Union sent rather large delegations (five and
six members each), while eight delegations had but a single member.
The International Telecommunication Union (ITU) was represented
through its deputy secretary and three further observers; the UN Educational, Scientific and Cultural Organization (UNESCO) sent one
observer.[44]

The professional background of the heads of the delegations can
be subsumed under four categories:

1. Diplomats: members of the diplomatic corps, a member of the
   country's permanent mission to the United Nations (usually second
   secretary or counselor), or officials from the foreign ministry.

2. Scientists: engineers, space researchers, space administrators.
3. Politicians/administrators: usually lawyers; officials from ministries of communications, post and telecommunications, and so on.
4. Broadcasters: professionals in broadcasting.

At this working group meeting, 11 delegations were headed by
diplomats (50 percent), 6 by scientists (27 percent), 4 by politicians/
administrators (18 percent) and 1 by a broadcaster (5 percent).[45]
The working group received official papers from Sweden and
Canada, the United States, ITU,[46] and UNESCO.
The Swedish-Canadian working paper stated that satellite broadcasting is, as all other space activities, inherently international, or
planetary, in character, it therefore requires action at the same level.
The penalty for failing to act will be severe; not only will a lack of
action compromise the interests of countries, individually or collectively, it may also lead to a chaotic situation, thereby impairing relations
between countries. The paper, then, stressed the necessity for international cooperation and coordinated international arrangements. The
possible arrangements which merit detailed study can be classified as
follows:

1. Political: to ensure the use of satellite broadcasting in the public
   interest, for peaceful purposes, and for better understanding between nations and to secure the availability of this service to all
   states, on a global and nondiscriminatory basis.
2. Technical: to ensure the orderly, efficient, and equitable use of
   the radio-frequency spectrum, to promote the harmonious integration of satellite broadcasting facilities with present and planned
   telecommunication requirements, and to secure compatibility of
   spectrum usage, including orbital positions and freedom from interference.
3. Economic: to ensure availability of satellite broadcasting to all
   states, developed and developing, irrespective of the stage of
   their individual social, economic, and technical characteristics.
4. Administrative: to encourage organizational and administrative
   forms providing equitable access to broadcasting satellite systems.
5. Cultural: to assist the free flow of education, scientific, cultural,
   and informational material and to promote favorable conditions for
   the mass media to collect, provide, and exchange news, programs,
   and program materials.
6. Aid: to assist developing countries to take full advantage of this
   new technology.
7. Legal: to provide in such arrangements as are required an equitable
   means of settling any disputes, adequate protection, if necessary,
   of various kinds of rights, and a harmonization of differing legal
   rules concerning these rights.[47]

The U.S. working paper limited itself to a discussion of the technical feasbility of television broadcasting from satellites and established the previously mentioned classification that distinguishes (1) primary (principal) grade of service, (2) secondary (rural) grade of service, and (3) community grade of service.[48]

The International Telecommunication Union in a working paper described ITU's function with respect to direct broadcast satellites as being threefold:

1. Proper integration of all space telecommunications with conventional terrestrial techniques and systems.
2. Effective and interference-free operation between all the service usages to which radio communications are put in space and on earth.
3. Cooperation as an executive agent either as a general advisor or by way of actually establishing and introducing new techniques and facilities—for the new and developing countries.[49]

ITU Deputy Secretary general R. E. Butler placed particular emphasis on this organization's responsibility in regard to technological innovation: "It was and continues to be an absolute duty for the ITU under its charter, to look on to the new aspects raised in its field of competence."[50]

The final report of the working group, then, summarized the considerations on the technical feasbility of communication by direct broadcasts from satellites and the current and foreseeable developments in this field by establishing the now-famous timetable for future developments of the three basic types of direct satellite broadcasting:

Direct broadcast into community receivers could be close at hand. Technology currently under development might allow this in the mid-1970s.

Direct broadcast of television into augmented home receivers could become feasible technologically as soon as 1975.

Direct broadcasting of television into existing, unaugmented home receivers on an operational basis is not foreseen for the period 1970-1985.[51]

As for the costs of these systems, the report came to the following conclusion. Taking the cost of existing unaugmented receivers as a reference, and assuming mass production of the order of a million or more units, the extra cost per receiving installation was estimated, for direct-to-home television broadcasting using augmented receivers, at $40 to $270 (U.S.); and, for television broadcasting to community or collective receiving arrangements, at $150.[52]

The Second Meeting:
July–August 1969

The Working Group on Direct Broadcast Satellites held its second
session at the UN office at Geneva between July 28 and August 7, 1969,
under the chairmanship of Rydbeck (Sweden). The working group held
nine meetings.

Of the 28 member states of the parent committee (the Committee
on the Peaceful Uses of Outer Space), 22 states were represented at
the meetings. The average delegation consisted of 2.9 representatives
and advisors. The largest delegations were sent by Italy (eight members), Brazil (six), and the United States (five), while four states sent
only one-man delegations. The ITU was represented by four observers,
UNESCO by two.[53]

According to the previously developed classification scheme of
the professional background of the heads of delegations, the picture
at the second meeting was the following: eleven delegations were
headed by diplomats (50 percent), six by politicians/administrators
(27 percent), three by scientists (14 percent), and two by broadcasters
(9 percent).[54]

The working group received official papers on DBS from Argentina,
Australia, Canada and Sweden, Czechoslovakia, France, Mexico, and
the United Kingdom, and from UNESCO, and heard the statements of
several delegations on the matter.[55]

The Swedish–Canadian working paper started out by addressing
itself to the question of the applicability of international law to direct
satellite broadcasting. Three principles enshrined in Article I of the
Outer Space Treaty, the two delegations held, were directly applicable:
(1) "free use in conformity with international law," (2) "sovereign
equality of states" and (3) "common interest of all mankind." In broader terms, they concluded that "it seems reasonable to suggest, therefore, that sovereignty and state responsibility, international co-operation and mutuality of interests, are likely to be major principles of
international law relating to direct satellite broadcasting."[56]

The working paper, then, suggested several practical measures
designed to make possible and promote the best use of direct broadcast satellites:

1. Agreement on frequency allocations and technical coordination procedures for direct satellite broadcasting within the framework of the
   ITU (the ITU took up this issue at its 1971 World Administrative
   Radio Conference on Space Communications).
2. Improved coordination among those international organizations which
   have an important role to play in the development of DBS and whose
   present activities will be affected by it.

3. International arrangements to facilitate the orderly development of
regional and international cooperative programming undertaken by
individual broadcasting organizations within the jurisdictional
framework of the state authorities.[57]

The U.K. working paper consisted largely of a general description
of the various problems generated by DBS. It recognized that different
political, social, cultural, economic environments were likely to lead
to disputes over the content of program material. While some content
might be acceptable in one country it may be offensive in others and
wide variations in culture and social customs may generate friction.[58]
The only direct suggestion made in the paper had to do with commercial advertising by means of direct broadcast satellites:

> DBS is a potent tool for commercial advertising and
> could lead to significant changes in trading patterns par-
> ticularly if a few space powers achieve a monopolistic
> position. If international television advertising were to
> be permitted, common international codes of practice in
> commercial advertising would be desirable.[59]

The Australian delegation assumed a similar position. It suggested
that the efforts of the working group might be directed towards the
preparation of a basic code of program standards for international transmissions. Among other things, the advertising content of programs
would "probably need to be covered in the basic code."[60] Without
making a concrete proposal, the Australian working paper foresaw
difficulties in a number of countries that have certain domestic requirements such as a specific minimum proportion of locally produced
material or general import controls on broadcast programs.[61]

The French working paper was the first to contain specific suggestions as to a framework of regulation of DBS. Recognizing the "un-
deniable advantages" of this new technology, the paper was more concerned with possible hazards. As the technological resources would
be beyond the means of all but a small number of states, "the economic
and technological inequality of the members of the international community will thus be confirmed anew, in a particularly striking fashion."[62] This inequality would further increase the possibility of interference in the internal affairs of foreign states, and national culture,
civilizations, and social systems would be presented with a further
means of imposing themselves on others through the suggestive power
of television.[63] The working paper does not, therefore, consider the
principle of freedom of information as legally binding in international
law. "If the use of direct broadcast satellites is accepted by the international community, the principles of freedom of space and freedom
of information can only be applied subject to appropriate international
legislation."[64]

Against the background of this general political attitude, the French delegation, then, proposed:

1. All states whose territory is affected by the broadcasts should be entitled to use the radio transmitters installed in the satellites on fair and reasonable terms.
2. The broadcasting of advertisements without the consent of the state on whose territory the broadcasts can be received should be prohibited.
3. A code of conduct should be developed, including a ban of broadcasts containing, inter alia, propaganda, interference in international affairs of other states, objectionable elements likely to disturb the balance of culture, religion, and philosophy, and tendentious information.
4. A right of reply should be established.
5. International means of supervision should be considered.[65]

The Czechoslovakian working paper stressed the recognition of General Assembly Resolution 110 of 1947 that prohibited propaganda, and the responsibility of states for activities in outer space and the need for international cooperation.[66] The Mexican delegation expressed its concern for the fact that DBS was likely to be accessible only to the highly developed countries.[67]

The statement by UNESCO, which has observer status at the United Nations, reported on the various UNESCO activities with regard to satellite communication. It stressed the recognition that the introduction of space communication occurs in widely different socioeconomic, technological, and cultural environments[68] and the need to avoid program material which is considered objectionable by the public in certain countries or areas.[69]

At its second session, the working group considered the implications of DBS in the social, cultural, legal, and other areas. In its report, the working group delineated the areas of agreement between the members and those that needed further study. The working group considered that even though the technical feasibility predictions contained in its first report indicate that a number of the problems discussed might not come to a head for some years, nevertheless there was a need to continue studies in the intervening period with a view to completing, where possible, satisfactory international arrangements.[70]

As for the applicability of international law, the working group noted the existence of a number of international legal instruments which would apply to direct broadcasts from satellites, including the UN Charter, the Outer Space Treaty, and the ITU Convention and Radio Regulations. Concerning the content of broadcasts, the report could only note that considerable difficulties lay in the way of producing a generally acceptable code which might govern the content of direct broadcasts from satellites, "having regard to the different standards of program acceptability which exist in different States, these standards having a close relationship to the levels of accepted social customs and practices in respective States."[71] The report further noted the role that broadcasting organizations were playing in developing new patterns of cooperation in broadcasting, using existing means of tele-communications, including satellites, which could be significant for future direct broadcasting from satellites.

Finally, the working group believed that it could, if continued, play a useful role in helping to coordinate and study various matters related to DBS. The Outer Space Committee recommended then to the General Assembly the continuation of the mandate of the working group. The General Assembly approved the continuance of the mandate.[72]

The Third Meeting:
May 1970

The Working Group on Direct Broadcast Satellites held its third session at the UN headquarters, in New York, between May 11 and May 21, 1970, under the chairmanship of Rydbeck (Sweden). Nine meetings were held during this session.

Of the 28 member states of the parent committee, 25 states were represented at the meetings. The average delegation consisted of 2.5 representatives and advisors. The largest delegations were sent by the United States (ten members), Canada (six), and the Soviet Union (five). Ten delegations consisted only of one representative. UNESCO sent two observers, while the ITU, the World Meteorological Organization, and the United International Bureau for the Protection of Intellectual Property were represented by one observer each.[73]

In accordance with the previously developed classification scheme of the professional background of the heads of delegations, the distribution at the third session was the following: Eighteen delegations were headed by diplomats (72 percent), four by scientists (16 percent), two by politicians/administrators (8 percent), and one by a broadcaster (4 percent).[74]

This meeting was basically an extension of the second session (of 1969): like that session it considered the "implications of direct broadcast satellites in social, cultural, legal and other areas, as well as the principles which would underlie and promote international cooperation in this field."[75] The working group received working papers from Canada/Sweden, the Soviet Union, and France.[76]

Introducing the joint Swedish-Canadian paper,[77] the Canadian delegate drew a distinction between hardware and software of direct satellite broadcasting. As to software, the paper pointed out that certain countries feared that such broadcasts might be used for purposes unacceptable for receiving countries, and others feared "cultural

intrusion." The joint study discussed such suggestions as, that no
program should be beamed over the territory of a state without its consent. However, the delegate said, "these were only tentative suggestions and others might prove more fruitful."[78] The problem of content
of broadcasts, the paper said, would be settled more easily if as many
countries as possible had access to the direct broadcast satellite system. Thus, the problems of hardware and programming of software were
directly linked. If access to a system were open to all, the probability
that a state would refuse to accept broadcasts would be reduced.[79]
The main conclusions of the joint paper were that direct satellite broadcasting would become technically feasible in the immediate future; that
the need for wide international cooperation should be recognized; and
that the concerns of states regarding programs could best be met through
participation at a regional level in the establishment and operation of
regional satellite broadcast systems.[80]

The Swedish delegate also stressed the necessity for a planned and
coordinated approach and considered cooperation and agreement a sine
qua non.[81] He further said that work in the field of direct satellite
broadcasting should be placed within the larger complex of studies on
various types of pollution of the environments. He mentioned pollution
of the seabed, the air, and outer space, and stated that though they
were dissimilar, they nevertheless had similarities which should be
studied.[82]

The French delegate introduced his delegation's working paper entitled "Proposed Principles to Govern Direct Broadcasts from Communications Satellites"[83] and said that to neglect consideration of the law
which should govern direct broadcast satellites would be like setting
in motion "a vehicle without a wheel." He observed that the development of space law lagged behind technology, and said that it was
necessary to ensure that "the development of a new technology does
not become a factor of discord among nations"; to avoid "dangers of
anarchical development," states must seek a common philosophy concerning this new means of communication.[84]

The French paper suggested two general principles to govern activities in this field: First, every state was free to make use of satellites
for broadcasting, in conformity with the rules of international law and
the UN Charter, but there must be respect for the sovereignty of states
which did not want their territory covered by such broadcasts. Second,
every state whose territory was covered by a satellite should be able
to use the satellite transmitters for its own benefit under equitable
and reasonable terms.[85]

The paper provided for a prohibition of intervention into the domestic affairs of states or the conduct of their foreign policy; material
offensive to a head of state or government or to other officials; any
propaganda likely to interfere with international or national peace;
material tending to incite a violation of human rights; anything likely
to shock a people's moral or philosophical beliefs; and scenes of
violence. Broadcasts to children should not be such as to harm their

development, and those intended for adults should be accompanied by announcements identifying their nature. Broadcasts should respect the civilizations, religions, and philosophies of the region receiving them.[86]

The paper suggested several principles to govern advertising by direct broadcast satellite: that advertising should be allowed only with the prior agreement of the state concerned; that it should be kept separate from noncommercial material; that it should preferably be of an artistic or educational nature; that it should not exploit the lack of experience or knowledge of the consumer or mislead him; and that it should avoid defamatory illusions or statements which could bring about monetary loss to someone.[87]

Similarly, the USSR working paper[88] proposed the elaboration of legal principles which should include the following: direct satellite broadcasts must be in the interest of progress, mutual understanding, and friendly relations: they must be conducted by states on the basis of recognized international law; cooperation in direct satellite broadcasts can be carried out only on the basis of strict adherence to the principles of national sovereignty, equal rights, nondiscrimination and peaceful coexistence; direct satellite broadcasts to foreign countries can be made only with the explicit agreement of the governments of the receiving countries. Also, the broadcasts must be carried out for the purpose of raising the educational level and increasing international exchanges. Illegal broadcasts containing propaganda for national and racial hatred or obscene material should be ruled out. The responsibility of states for such broadcasts must be established.[89]

While UNESCO was essentially concerned with the positive aspects of using the new technology for education, science, and culture, its delegate nevertheless pointed out that "we are aware of the dangers and the risks, and the possibilities of misuse of what is probably the most powerful instrument ever available to man for the communication of ideas."[90] Not only should satellite broadcasts be avoided which may be offensive to the beliefs and customs of recipients, but "we should also guard against the more subtle dangers of a flood of program material, foreign to a nation's spirit and values, that may, in time, lead to cultural extinction."[91]

Various statements were made by other delegations in the general debate. Argentina stressed the necessity for striking a balance between the freedom to transmit information and the needs of the international community by establishing a principle of prior consent. Belgium cautioned of hasty conclusions as the speed of technological development could not yet be assessed, and contended that the question of spillover of broadcasts did not present any major difficulties. Belgium, its delegate said, even benefited from that phenomenon. Mexico and Italy were concerned about equal access and space monopoly by the superpowers and Brazil held that there was the danger of establishing "a position of privilege" for one nation.[92]

Differences of opinion arose also with respect to the significance of the distinction between reception by community receivers and in-

dividual receivers. The United States, Belgium, and the United Kingdom suggested that the working group should concern itself exclusively with DBS to community receivers, as this was the only technology
feasible at the time, while the USSR, France, and Czechoslovakia
contended that the same principles should apply to both community
and individual receivers. In the words of the USSR delegate: "The
development of technology will lead to the gradual disappearance of
such distinction. There is certainly no legal or social distinction between the two."93

The basic difference between these two positions extended to the
more fundamental question of whether the elaboration of principles was
appropriate at all. While a majority of delegations—to varying degrees—
supported the basic idea of a certain measure of regulation, the United
Kingdom and the United States felt that to draft such principles would
be premature. The U.K. delegate thought it "could limit freedom where
it already existed, such as in the case of radio broadcasts."94 The
United States expressed its doubts whether a study of principles in
itself could contribute to the improvement of international cooperation.
Existing regulations should be studied first; a premature study of "hypothetically feasible" means of communication could give rise to con-
fusion. "This might not improve co-operation but, on the contrary,
might increase the existing gap."95

In its third report, the working group stated that it had completed
the work that it could usefully effect at this stage. It suggested that
the Outer Space Committee consider the reconvening of the group when
further material of substance was available, mainly as a result of work
done in the same field by UNESCO and ITU.96

The working group also concluded that there are no known programs
of broadcasting satellite services for individual reception, but that
such broadcasts for community receivers would be feasible in the near
future. The report referred to the importance of satellite-borne television for educational and training purposes, particularly for developing countries, where it could contribute to national programs of integration and community development, as well as to economic and social
development.97

The working group in its conclusions, also recognized that such
satellite broadcasting services require broad international cooperation
and, in this connection, it noted the existence of a number of international instruments relevant to the field. The report adds that improve-
ments in space technology would lead to lessening the concern of
countries receiving such broadcasts because more precise antenna
pointing and shaping of beams could avoid interference and spillover
of transmissions into countries not wanting to receive them. The
report stressed the desirability of regional cooperation in satellite
broadcasting and recommended that regional cooperation be promoted
both on the governmental and the nongovernmental level, especially
among broadcasters and their associations.98

Another recommendation called for member states, the United Nations Development Program, and other international bodies to assist developing countries in benefiting from satellite broadcasting and in developing the skills and techniques for its application. Developing countries should be assisted in determining whether direct satellite broadcasting systems were the best means to satisfy their broadcasting requirements and, if so, to give sympathetic consideration to their request for assistance.[99]

When the Outer Space Committee met from September 1 to September 17, 1970, in New York, it agreed to keep under review the question of reconvening the working group at such time as further material of substance may have become available on which further useful studies might be based.[100] The General Assembly endorsed this conclusion in Resolution 2733A which was adopted unanimously.[101]

DEVELOPMENTS IN 1971-72

Several developments occurred in the period of 1971-72 that produced the above mentioned "further material of substance"[102] which in turn led to the resumption of the working group meetings in 1973.

During these two years, the following actions were taken in regard to broadcasting from satellites:

1. The decision and recommendations adopted by the ITU at the World Administrative Radio Conference for Space Telecommunications, in Geneva in 1971; these decisions, upon ratification, were in force as of January 1, 1973. The recommendations dealt with the allocation of frequencies for all kinds of space communications, including satellite broadcasting, as well as with the technical and administrative regulations concerning the establishment and operation of satellite communication systems. (The results of the WARC (space), 1971, as they regard DBS, have been discussed in Chapter 1.)

2. The request by the Soviet Union on August 11, 1972, to include in the agenda of the 1972 General Assembly the question of the elaboration of an international convention on principles governing the use by states of artificial earth satellites for direct television broadcasting.[103]

3. The decision of the Outer Space Committee at its meeting of September 1972 to reconvene the Working Group on Direct Broadcast Satellites in 1973.[104]

4. The adoption of General Assembly Resolution 2916 of November 9, 1972, in which the General Assembly requested the Outer Space Committee to "undertake as soon as possible the elaboration of principles governing the use by states of artificial earth satellites for direct television broadcasting with a view to concluding an international agreement or agreements."[105]

5. The adoption of the UNESCO Declaration of Guiding Principles on
   the Use of Satellite Broadcasting for the Free Flow of Information,
   the Spread of Education and Greater Cultural Exchange, on November 15, 1972.[106]

The Initiative of the Soviet Union

In a letter to the secretary general of the United Nations dated
August 8, 1972, the foregin minister of the Soviet Union, Andrei
Gromyko, requested the inclusion in the agenda of the twenty-seventh
session of the General Assembly of a separate item: "Preparation of
an international convention on principles governing the use by States
of artificial earth satellites for direct television broadcasting."[107]
He pointed out that the transmission of television programs by means
of satellites directly to home television receivers (direct television
broadcasting) is one of the most promising potential uses of space to
meet man's needs, while at the same time, he noted, it will raise
serious legal problems connected with the need to establish conditions
under which this new form of space technology will serve only "the
lofty goals of peace and friendship between peoples."[108]
Attached to the letter was the first draft convention to be elaborated on DBS. In addition to eight preambular paragraphs, it contained
17 comprehensive articles covering the whole range of legal aspects
surrounding this new technology. The following six basic elements
should suffice to describe the general thrust of the Soviet draft convention which concentrates on direct television broadcasting:

1. Direct television broadcasting is to be carried out exclusively in
   the interests of peace, progress, the development of mutual understanding, and the strengthening of friendly relations between
   peoples, and should serve the goals of enhancing the educational
   level of the population, developing culture, and expanding international exchanges.
2. All states must have an equal right to carry out direct television
   broadcasting and to enjoy the benefits arising from that form of
   broadcasting, without discrimination of any kind.
3. Direct television broadcasting to foreign states is to be carried
   out only with the express consent of the latter.
4. The following types of broadcasts are to be regarded as illegal
   and as incurring international liability: broadcasts made to other
   states without their express consent, broadcasts detrimental to
   the maintenance of international peace and security, broadcasts
   which represent interference in the domestic affairs of states or
   encroachment on fundamental human rights, and broadcasts which
   propagandize violence and horrors, undermine the foundations of
   the local civilization and culture, or misinform the public.

5. States may utilize the means at their disposal in order to counter-
act illegal direct television broadcasting of which they are the
object, not only in their own territory but also in outer space and
other areas beyond the limits of the national jurisdiction of any
state.

6. A state must bear responsibility for all national direct television
broadcasting activities, irrespective of whether the broadcasting
is carried out by governmental agencies or by nongovernmental
organizations and juridical persons.[109]

General Assembly Debate and
Resolution 2916

The initiative of the Soviet Union of August 1972 led to a wide-
ranging debate on direct broadcast satellites in the First Committee
of the General Assembly during October 12–October 20, 1972. These
discussions concerned themselves with the generalities of the Soviet
draft convention, its underlying ideas and philosophical questions
associated with the emergence of this new communications technology.
Finally, this debate provided the basis for the adoption of General
Assembly Resolution 2916 of November 9, 1972, that requested the
Outer Space Committee to elaborate principles governing the use of
direct broadcast satellites with a view to concluding an international
agreement. (For the full text of Resolution 2916 see Appendix B.)

This section's purpose is to highlight the essentials of this debate which can be grouped around three areas of concern: (1) freedom
of information and the protection of national sovereignty; (2) imbalance
of power between space nations and others and the issue of cultural
identity; (3) appropriateness of regulation prior to technological feasibility.

The first group of statements regarding freedom of information was
introduced by the U.S. delegate who thought the Soviet proposal would
present difficult problems because it would affect very fundamental
principles to which the United States and other countries attached
cardinal importance. "I refer to our strong 200–year–old belief in
the free exchange of information and ideas. A primary basis for the
maintenance of democratic institutions is the continuing application
of this principle, which is also, of course, enshrined in the United
Nations Charter."[110]

The U.K. delegation pointed out that the principle of the free flow
of information was "fundamental to our way of life" and Australia held
that any regulation of the direct broadcast satellite should not curb
the free flow of information and knowledge around the world.[111]

The delegate of Belgium used the strongest language against the
proposals of the Soviet Union. Not wishing "in any way to hide" his
delegation's "hesitation," he was

Surprised to note that nowhere in the Soviet proposal
is the sacred principle of freedom of information affirmed.
Not to mention freedom of information at all can lead to
excessive abuse that is contrary to the principles laid down
in the Charter of the United Nations.[112]

As in earlier statements, Belgium explained its own domestic situation
as being covered by broadcasts from five neighboring countries. It was
found that without undue regulations, Belgium has been able to accept
these television programs without any fear and without any harm to its
people.[113]

This particular emphasis on the principle of freedom of information
by the delegate of Belgium prompted the Soviet Union and other Socialist
countries to produce their own definition of this principle:

Mr. Malik (USSR): Further, the representative of Belgium
spoke of the free flow of information. But a question arises,
whose flow? A clean flow, a creative flow in the interests
of peace and mankind? Or is it to be polluted by sex, violence, propaganda, misinformation, slander, interference
in international affairs, against the culture and civilization
of every single nation? This is what we are talking about.[114]

The Chilean delegate saw in "what is known as 'freedom of information' a false conception that seeks to consolidate the exploita-
tion of the masses,"[115] while the Polish statement represented the
case for protection: "The cultural environment of nations, like the
biological natural environment, requires protection from hatred and
abuse, which is but another kind of pollution that endangers and
stifles international co-operation and detente."[116]

The Mexican delegation made a distinction between domestic and
international communications. While believing in the "absolute freedom of information" within national frontiers, it contended that, from
an international standpoint, the principle of the sovereignty of the
state "must curtail the application of the principle of the free flow
of information."[117]

This and similar positions were taken by a number of states. While
recognizing the need for safeguarding the rights of the receiving state,
they also felt that there was no contradiction between the concept of
national sovereignty and the principle of the free flow of information
and that a balance has to be struck between the two. Statements to
this effect were made by the delegations of Iran, Brazil, Austria,
India, Indonesia, and Argentina.[118]

Regarding the second group of issues which had to do with the
relationship between space nations and developing countries, the
statement by the delegate of Pakistan best summarized the concerns
of the emerging nations:

Unlike wireless broadcasting, satellite telecasting
will be, and is likely to remain, the preserve of only a
handful of technologically advanced and economically
affluent countries. It may, therefore, accentuate the
cultural and intellectual gulf which is already beginning
to widen between the developed and the less developed
parts of our globe. We would suggest, therefore, that
ways should be examined of enabling the developing
countries to share in the use of television satellites.[119]

The same note was struck by such nations as Iran and Chile that also
emphasized the need to preserve the originality of cultures.[120] This
concern received support from some industrialized countries, especially
the Soviet Union and France.[121]

The third group of issues related to the timeliness of regulation.
The United States repeatedly stressed the fact that direct satellite
broadcasting to unaugmented home receivers would not become technically feasible until 1985 and that, therefore, there was no "adequate
basis for trying to draw up definitive international arrangements."[122]
This view was shared by the delegations of the United Kingdom, Australia, and Belgium.[123]

On the other side, some nations rejected the notion of prematurity
on the basis of the philosophical consideration that new technology
should follow, not precede, new law;[124] while others feared a "sudden
technological breakthrough that could catch us unaware and unprepared."[125]

As a result of the First Committee debate, the final draft of General Assembly Resolution 2916 emerged. It stressed the need for some
type of principles governing the use of direct satellite broadcasting.
When the resolution came up for the vote in the plenary on November
9, 1972, the U.S. delegation explained the reasons that impelled it
to cast a negative vote: First, "The resolution does not sufficiently
take note of the positive potential of what we foresee as the new technology involved in the use of earth satellites for direct television
broadcasting." Second, " . . . It does not put sufficient emphasis on
the central importance of the free flow of information and ideas in the
modern world." While the United States was prepared now to take
part in an international study on direct satellite broadcasting, it
could not agree—"in advance of substantive work"—that the "results
of this study should take a particular form. Specifically, we are not
ready at this juncture to agree that the goal of the study ought to be
either principles or a treaty."[126]

The General Assembly, then, adopted Resolution 2916 by a vote
of 102 to 1 (the United States) with 7 abstentions.[127]

The UNESCO Declaration on
Satellite Broadcasting

One of the new substantive materials available cited by the Outer
Space Committee report of 1972 was the Declaration of Guiding Principles on the Use of Satellite Broadcasting for the Free Flow of Information, the Spread of Education and Greater Cultural Exchange by the 17th
General Conference of UNESCO on November 17, 1972. The 11-article
declaration which is not binding on governments, was adopted by a
vote of 55 (including the USSR) to 7 (including the United States) with
22 abstentions.[128]

The philosophy of the declaration was restrictive, stressing sovereignty, the requirement that news broadcasts be accurate, the right
of each country to decide the contents of education programs broadcast to it, the need for broadcasters to respect cultural distinctiveness
and varied laws, and the requirement for prior consent especially regarding advertising.[129]

THE WORKING GROUP ON
DIRECT BROADCAST SATELLITES:
1973-74

The Fourth Meeting
June 1973

The Working Group on Direct Broadcast Satellites held its fourth
session at the UN headquarters, in New York, from June 11 to June
22, 1973, under the chairmanship of Rydbeck (Sweden). The working
group held 17 meetings.

Of the 28 member states of the parent committee, 24 states were
represented at the meetings. The average delegation consisted of three
representatives and advisors. The largest delegations were sent by
the United States (eleven members), Japan (six) and the Soviet Union
(five); five delegations consisted of but one representative. The International Telecommunication Union sent two observers, while UNESCO
and the Food and Agriculture Organization were represented by one
observer each.[130]

In accordance with the previously developed classification scheme
of the professional background of the heads of delegations, the distribution at the fourth session was the following: nineteen delegations
were headed by diplomats (79 percent), three by politicians/administra-
tors (13 percent), one by a scientist (4 percent), and one by a broadcaster (4 percent).[131]

The working group received working papers by Canada/Sweden and by the United States as well as the draft conventions proposed by the Soviet Union on principles governing the use by states of artificial earth satellites for direct television broadcasting.[132]

The Canadian–Swedish working paper came to three basic conclusions: First, there are no known requirements or plans for systems providing worldwide coverage for individual, direct-to-home reception. Second, in the light of the ITU regulations of 1971, the basic technical and regulatory level provides for continuous information and coordination between all states concerned and accordingly there are ample opportunities for states to object against actions which might be deemed harmful to their interests. Third, it would appear advisable at this stage for the working group to address itself to the elaboration of the general principles which should govern direct television broadcasting by satellite.[133]

The delegations of Canada and Sweden, then, submitted a proposal of principles governing direct television broadcasting by satellite. This draft differed in some important parts from the Soviet proposal of 1972. While it also supported the principles of "consent" and "participation"[134] it made a distinction between intentional coverage of a foreign territory and coverage which is technically unavoidable, that is, spillover: The consent obligation would apply only to cases of technically unavoidable spillover.[135] Moreover, Canada and Sweden felt that "given the political, economic, social, and cultural differences among states, it would appear extremely difficult or impossible to obtain general agreement on certain types of provisions—for example, those dealing with program content."[136]

In addition, the joint proposal did not contain any provision for unilateral remedial action in the case of violations but stressed international cooperation and consultations.[137] The position that the principles of national sovereignty and free flow of information are not mutually exclusive—a position pronounced on many occasions by the two sponsor countries as well as by other delegations—found its clear expression in Article II of this proposal:

> Direct television broadcasting by satellite shall be carried out in a manner compatible with the maintenance of international peace and security, the development of mutual understanding and the strengthening of friendly relations among all States and peoples. Such broadcasting shall also be conducted on the basis of respect for the principles of the sovereignty of States, non-intervention and equality and in the interest of promoting the free flow of communications.[138]

Although the Canadian delegate pointed out that his delegation did not think in terms of a "worst case" scenario for the development of this new form of technology, he hinted at certain concerns that may explain his country's support of the prior consent principle:

> To put the issue in its simplest terms; should a foreign country or an enterprise outside of Canada be given the right to establish for Canada and without out consent, a new television broadcasting system, in effect a fourth system, in competition with existing national networks, this could be highly damaging to the tremendous investments which have been made in the existing Canadian broadcasting infrastructure.[139]

As to the form that the principles should take, the Canadian delegate thought it would be unwise to proceed with haste in developing legal rules in binding treaty form. The international community has not yet gained sufficient experience with the technology—particularly with direct broadcasting to home receivers which will not be a reality for years—to be able to issue hard and fast rules that could only be modified or altered by the very complex process that treaty amendment entails.[140] Rather, he suggested, it would be more appropriate at this time if a body of principles were to be declared by the UN General Assembly as governing direct satellite broadcasting activities, in a manner not unlike the 1963 declaration on principles governing the use of outer space, which preceded the Outer Space Treaty.[141]

The United States submitted a working paper on a number of technical questions. It stressed the fact that no work was going on in the United States to develop a direct-to-home satellite system while "all work to date in the United States and Canada has concentrated on development of a capability for community broadcasting or television distribution."[142] The paper also suggested "a formal finding by the Working Group that no one is doing any work now on the development of a capability for direct (as opposed to community) television broadcasting from satellites, and thus no projection can reasonably be made concerning a readiness date for such technology."[143]

The statement by the U.S. delegate reiterated these facts and pointed out that "broadcast to community systems, of course, should arouse none of the concerns apparently perceived by some countries in relation to systems utilizing individual home receivers without utilizing a ground station or other intermediary for retransmission."[144] The United States opposed the elaboration of principles at this meeting on both substantive and procedural grounds. Procedurally, its position was that the Legal Subcommittee of the Outer Space Committee, as the expert body for legal matters in the Outer Space Committee family, should be given the opportunity to analyze and comment on these principles.[145] As to the substantive issues involved, the U.S. delegation thought it would be wrong to attempt to establish globally applicable principles concerning a technology which is still far in the future and may be regionally organized if it does come into being. It noted that as far as the United States was concerned, the broadcasters have shown no interest in developing a domestic direct broadcast satellite television system. The existing infrastructure of the present U.S. television system was too broad, and represented too great an investment, to be replaced economically be telecasting in a different mode, even if this was technically feasible.[146]

Another aspect of the U.S. position was that it would be unwise to run the risk of inhibiting technical progress by freezing international behavior in connection with satellite broadcasts at an unduly early state. "We believe that we must have a clearer picture of what it is we are dealing with and, indeed, what concrete and specific problems are foreseen in the use of the technology before we establish principles designed to govern it."[147]

The American delegate, then, reiterated his delegation's concern regarding the constitutional commitment to the principle of freedom of speech. He quoted Justice Wendell Holmes who expressed this fundamental value in these words: ". . . the ultimate good desired is better reached by free trade in ideas . . . the best test of truth is the power of the thought to get itself accepted in the competition of the market. . . . "[148] The U.S. position was that in the competition of the market of thought and ideas, the freedom to receive information was just as important as the freedom to impart it, and the delegation saw in the principle of prior consent an inherent danger of sanctioning not only total censorship "but such arbitrary and diverse application of the principle as to nullify the basic human right to exchange ideas and information."[149]

As to the fear that the free flow of information and ideas might be a one-way flow controlled by the few powers technically capable of launching, and financially able to operate, a satellite service, the United States was prepared to study possible arrangements for sharing broadcast time and channels on any future direct broadcast system among countries within a given region.[150]

However, the U.S. statement did not want to exclude further study regarding possible regional approaches to arrangements facilitating the use of direct broadcast satellites. It also mentioned as warranting further exploration the adoption of voluntary codes of conduct by broadcasting unions.[151]

The statements made during the general debate[152] can be grouped around the following areas: appropriateness of principles in general, freedom of information, and cultural protection. In essence, the discussion was a reflection of the various lines of thought that emerged during the First Committee debate of October/November 1972.

The concept of prematurity of regulation was advanced by Belgium which thought it would be "dangerous to envision international laws without knowledge of what was to come," and by Japan whose delegate warned of "eager but over-hasty decisions" as well as by the United

Kingdom, Italy, and the United States. This concept was disputed by the delegations of Mexico, which opposed the idea of a "legal vacuum" regarding DBS, Brazil, and the Soviet Union.

The delegations of Belgium, the United Kingdom, and Japan placed a strong emphasis on the concept of freedom of information as a universally applicable principle while France, Argentina, Poland, and the USSR stressed the need for cultural protection and strict respect of national sovereignty and, therefore, supported the principles of prior consent and participations in the one or the other form. As in previous discussions, a large group of delegations occuped an intermediate position of seeing no real contradiction between the principles of freedom of information and national sovereignty. This group was joined by Australia which in earlier sessions held a position closer to that of the U.S. group. Although this delegation supported the "maximum possible" freedom of communication, it would not dispute, however, that a state had legitimate cause for concern if a foreign state was deliberately to beam a program into its territory, notwithstanding objections. "Each state has the right, as an attribute of its sovereignty, to determine for itself what foreign programs might be beamed into its territory."

As to comments regarding the future course of action in procedural terms, the delegations that pushed the hardest for an expedient conclusion of a convention, namely, the Socialst countries of Eastern Europe and the Soviet Union, also suggested a shift of venue to the legal subcommittee which should commence the drafting of legal principles.

In the report[153] to its parent body, the Committee on the Peaceful Uses of Outer Space, the working group expressed the view that it should give its primary attention to relevant legal and political problems, while continuing to study new developments in satellite broadcasting technology and the economic factors concerned. The working group further expressed the view that another session of the working group should be held before June 1974, when the Legal Subcommittee of the Outer Space Committee was to meet again. The report further recommended that the working group should be requested to consider and discuss principles on the use by states of artificial earth satellites for direct television broadcasting, with a view to making specific recommendations for the work of the legal subcommittee in this field.

These recommendations were endorsed by both the Outer Space Committee and the General Assembly.[154]

The Fifth Meeting:
March 1974

The Working Group on Direct Broadcast Satellites held its fifth session at the UN office in Geneva, from March 11 to March 22, 1974,

under the chairmanship of Rydbeck (Sweden). The working group held
nine meetings.

The UN General Assembly at its twenty-eighth session in 1973 ad-
mitted nine new countries to the Committee on the Peaceful Uses of
Outer Space: Chile, the German Democratic Republic, the Federal
Republic of Germany, Indonesia, Kenya, Nigeria, Pakistan, Sudan,
Venezuela. The total number of the members is now thirty-seven.
Of these, thirty states attended the meetings. The average delegation
size was 2.5 representatives and advisors. The largest delegations
were sent by the United States (seven members), Japan (six) and
Canada (six), while eleven states sent only one-person delegations.
The ITU was represented by five observers, the World Intellectual
Property Organization (WIPO) by two, and UNESCO by one.[155]

According to the previously developed classification scheme of
the professional backgrounds of the heads of delegations, the picture
at the fifth meeting was the following: twenty-two delegations were
headed by a diplomat (73 percent), four by politicians/administrators
(13 percent), two by scientists (7 percent), and two by broadcasters
(7 percent).[156]

In addition to the materials submitted to the fourth session in 1973,
the working group had before it a working paper by Canada and Sweden,
a working paper presented by the United States containing draft principles on direct broadcast satellites, and one paper by Argentina.[157]

The joint Swedish-Canadian draft proposal is based on the assumption that there is no necessary contradiction between the concept of
the free flow of communication and the elaboration of principles designed to make this concept compatible with the rights of states and
the protection of their economic, social and cultural values. As in
the 1973 proposal of the two countries, the cornerstone of the joint
draft was the prior consent principle (Article V) that is linked to the
principle of participation (Article VIII). The draft does not contain
any provisions concerning program content as the principle of prior
consent would render such rules unnecessary.

The proposal submitted by the Soviet Union was a slightly modified version of its 1972 draft. Two alterations are noteworthy: First,
the USSR appeared to have abandoned the idea of a "convention" in
favor of "principles"; second, regarding remedial action in the case
of violation, Article IX provided now for "measures which are recognized
as legal under international law," a limitation not contained in the
1972 draft. According to one observer, the earlier Soviet draft was
deliberately made to contain expendable "giveaway" provisions and
phrasing, "drafted with the conscious knowledge that they would be
objectionable to Western interests and also go well beyond Soviet
needs."[158]

The United States too, modified its position. While in earlier
sessions the American delegation rejected the necessity and desirability of principles in general, it now presented eleven draft

principles[159] which, however, were not put in binding form. They contained references to the Universal Declaration of Human Rights (Article I), the right of access (Article V), international cooperation (Article VII) and the desirability of "taking into account differences among cultures" (Article IV). Introducing this draft, the U.S. delegate pointed out that his delegation continued to have serious reservations about the advisability of adopting binding principles governing direct satellite broadcasting. Considerably more analysis and experimentation were needed to arrive at a consensus on an international approach to such broadcasting. He noted that his delegation had, in its draft, tried to reflect common interests and areas of understanding among the members of the working group. In the view of his delegation, satellite broadcasting directly to unaugmented or augmented individual receivers was not likely to be operational prior to 1985. The United States, he said, had no such capability under development, on the drawing boards, or intended. His delegation continued to reject the principle of prior consent. The goal of the international community should be to derive from direct broadcasting the greatest possible benefits for all and not to risk discouraging or distorting its potential for good.[160]

As for the positions of the other countries, no substantial deviations from earlier-held attitudes could be detected. France said "law should win the race with technology"; Mexico "freedom of information is only a political thesis which has no binding force." Argentina and Brazil pushed for an early conclusion of an elaborate legal framework for philosophical consideration based on certain legal traditions; such countries as Austria and Australia continued to hold the middle position along the lines of the Canadian and Swedish efforts; Iran and India emphasized the need for prior consent on grounds of concern about cultural integrity and protection; and a group consisting of Belgium, Japan, Italy, and the United Kingdom continued to stress the free flow of information concept and pointed out the danger that the promising technological development of direct satellite broadcasting might be hampered by restrictive international legislation.

Of the new members of the Outer Space Committee, four made statements in the working group. The Federal Republic of Germany felt that the legal treatment of direct television broadcasting should be approached with extreme caution so as to ensure that a technological innovation considered good in principle was not impaired or even doomed to failure in the long run on account of hasty regulation. The principle of freedom of information seemed to the West German delegation to carry at least as much weight as other principles under consideration. Allowance would have to be made for the fact that broadcasting of radio and television programs beyond national boundaries had been generally accepted by the community of nations for many years. The principle of international cooperation together with that of freedom of information, should be the basis of any discussion.

The delegate of the German Democratic Republic emphasized that direct television broadcasting should be carried out exclusively in the interests of peace, progress, the development of mutual understanding, and the strengthening of friendly relations between all states and peoples. While recognizing equal rights for all states to enjoy the benefit of such broadcasting, he said, the right of states to act against illegal television broadcasting by measures recognized as legal under international law should also be recognized. In the opinion of his delegation, the working paper submitted by the delegation of the Soviet Union consituted the most comprehensive basis for the drafting of a joint set of principles. His delegation considered that the principle of non-interference in the internal affairs of other states was an absolutely necessary element of any acceptable solution.

The Indonesian delegate said that for his country, which is a nation composed of many islands and numerous ethnic groups, a satellite broadcasting system would seem to constitute an ideal instrument to knit together the diverse elements of its society and to bring immediate practical benefits to many of the more remote settlements. While Indonesia thus recognized the great benefits to be derived from direct satellite broadcasting, the delegate said, it was important also to recognize the potentially harmful and destructive effects to national sovereignty which might result from an uncontrolled flow of information. It was clearly necessary, he said, to formulate a method of dealing with abuses of freedom of information acceptable to all states if satellite broadcasting was to reach its full potential.

The delegate of Pakistan pointed out that the essential task of the working group was to work out recommendations which would protect the sovereign rights of individual states while at the same time promoting a new technology with obvious benefits for all. The problem of reconciling the principle of free flow of information with that of national sovereignty and nonintervention in the affairs of other states could, he said, be found in the concept of prior consent as embodied in the proposal made by Sweden and Canada.

The report[161] of the working group could achieve some measure of agreement on such issues as applicability of international law, rights and benefits of states, international cooperation, state responsibility, and the peaceful settlement of disputes. The crucial questions of prior consent, spillover, and program content, however, remained unresolved. Moreover, the working group could not come to a decision as to its further activities.

LEGAL SUBCOMMITTEE MEETINGS
OF 1974 AND 1975

In accordance with General Assembly Resolution 3182 of December 18, 1973, the Working Group on Direct Broadcast Satellites considered

and discussed principles on the use by states of artificial earth satellites for direct television broadcasting with a view to making specific
recommendations for the work of the legal subcommittee in this field.
Accordingly, when the legal subcommittee convened its thirteenth
session from May 6 to May 31, 1974, the issue of direct satellite broadcasting was placed on the agenda as item 4 ("The various implications
of space communications: report of the Working Group on Direct Broadcast Satellites.").

The subcommittee decided to discuss those principles on which
there was a high degree of consensus during the fifth session of the
Working Group on Direct Broadcast Satellites: applicability of international law; rights and benefits of states; international cooperation;
state responsibility; and peaceful settlement of disputes.

At the request of the parent committee the drafting work was continued at the fourteenth session of the legal subcommittee during February 10 to March 7, 1975, which produced fourteen draft principles.
(For the full text of these principles see Appendix A.) These principles
constitute the current state of the international legislative process
regarding the control of the direct broadcast satellite.

The 1975 Draft Principles

1. Purposes and objectives: All of the countries recognized that
direct television broadcasting by satellite should contribute to preserv-
ing international peace and security and to developing mutual understanding and strengthening friendly ties and cooperation among all
states and all peoples.162 Other purposes recognized were the fostering
of economic and social development, particularly of developing countries,
facilitating and widening the international exchange of information, promoting cultural exchanges, and improving the educational level of
peoples. It was also agreed that states should engage in direct television broadcasting by satellite only in a manner entirely compatible
with these aims.

2. Applicability of international law: It was unanimously agreed
that the following instruments of existing international law should form
the basis for the conduct of states in the organization of direct television broadcasting by satellite: the Charter of the United Nations,
the Outer Space Treaty of 1967, and the relevant provisions of the
International Telecommunication Convention and its radio regulations.
The United States and others (for example, the United Kingdom and
Belgium) asserted that the Universal Declaration of Human Rights was
applicable to activities in the field of DBS. Some nations also contended that the Declaration on Principles of International Law concerning
Friendly Relations and Co-operation among States, and the International
Covenant on Civil and Political Rights were also applicable.

3. Rights and benefits of states: There was general agreement that every state has an equal right to conduct and to authorize DBS activities and that all states should enjoy equitable sharing without discrimination in the benefits derived from such activities on mutually agreed terms including, subject to national legislation, access to the use of this technology. The Soviet Union desired an addition indicating that the activities authorized by a state would be conducted under its supervision which, of course, was unacceptable not only to the U.S. delegation but also to many other countries where all broadcasting is entrusted either to public organizations outside the state hierarchy or to private persons. The delegation of the Federal Republic of Germany insisted on the inclusion of individuals as also being entitled to the rights and benefits of DBS.

4. International cooperation: There was general agreement that DBS activities should be based on international cooperation and that such cooperation should be subject to appropriate arrangements between the states concerned and/or entities authorized by them.

5. State responsibility: It was generally recognized that states shall bear international responsibility for DBS activities carried out by an international organization, responsibility for compliance with these principles shall be borne both by the international organization and by states participating in such organization. This principle, of course, follows closely Article VI of the Outer Space Treaty of 1967 that was adopted unanimously.

6. Consent and participation: This principle lies at the heart of the controversy over DBS which found its expression in two alternative proposals. Alternative A supported by the majority of delegations including the Soviet Union, Canada, and Sweden, proposes that direct satellite broadcasts specifically aimed at a foreign state shall require the consent of that state. The consenting state shall have the right to participate in activities which involve coverage of its territory. Alternative A further provides that this principle shall not apply where coverage of the territory of a foreign state results from radiation of the satellite signal within the limits considered technically unavoidable under the radio regulations of the International Telecommunication Union.

Alternative B supported by the minority (inter alia the United States, Belgium, the Federal Republic of Germany) concedes that DBS may be subject to such restrictions imposed by the state carrying out or authorizing it as are compatible with the principle of freedom of expression, "which includes freedom to seek, receive and impart information and ideas of all kinds, regardless of frontiers." However, Alternative B expressly rejects the prior consent principle in paragraph two but it provides for consultations: "The consent of any State in which such broadcasting is received is not [emphasis added] required, but the State carrying it out or authorizing it should consult fully with any such receiving State which so requests concerning any restrictions to be imposed by the former State."

7. Spillover: This principle, too, produced two alternatives. Alternative A sponsored by the majority, provides that all technical means available shall be used to reduce, to the maximum extent practicable, the radiation over the territory of other countries. Alternative B sponsored, inter alia, by the United States, calls for the reduction to the minimum by all reasonable means of any unintended radiation of the territory of other countries. The delegations of the United Kingdom and the Federal Republic of Germany expressed doubts as to the practicability of this principle and suggested it to be dropped altogether.

8. Program content: No agreement was possible on the principle of program content. A majority of delegations including the Soviet Union, Canada, and Sweden, supported paragraph one that provides for cooperation regarding the production and interchange of programs. Paragraph two calls for appropriate agreements on which the broadcasting of advertising should be based. The principle also contained a list of types of programs that should be excluded from direct television by satellite, namely "material which is detrimental to the maintenance of international peace and security, which publicizes ideas of war, militarism, national and racial hatred and enmity between peoples, which is aimed at interfering in the domestic affairs of other states or which undermines the foundations of the local civilization, culture, way of life, traditions or language." For the most part, this principle is taken directly from the Soviet draft proposal and, therefore, found only limited acceptance.

9. Unlawful/inadmissible broadcasts: This principle, too, remained without agreement and is also based on Soviet ideas. It enumerates broadcasts that are in violation of one or more of the proposed principles and therefore illegal. It also provides that a state may take in respect to unlawful broadcasts measures which are recognized as legal under international law.

10. Duty and right to consult: The majority of delegations including the Soviet Union, Canada, and Sweden, supported Alternative A that provides that if a state has reason to believe that as a result of DBS activities carried out or authorized by other states it will be prejudicially affected by radiation over its territory, it may request that consultations be held and that a state receiving such a request shall enter into such consultations without delay. Alternative B, supported by the minority including the United States and the United Kingdom, calls for essentially the same procedure but uses weaker language: "Any State requested to do so by another State should without delay enter into consultations with the latter State concerning any matter arising from activities in the field of direct television broadcasting carried out or authorized by either of them which are likely to affect the other."

11. Peaceful settlement of disputes: Complete agreement could be reached that any disputes that may arise from DBS activities should be resolved by prompt consultations among the parties to such disputes.

Wide agreement could be achieved on the remaining three principles, that govern (12) copyright, (13) notification to the United Nations System, and (14) disruption. As to the first of them, it was held that states shall cooperate on a bilateral and multilateral basis for protection of copyright and neighboring rights by means of appropriate agreements between the interested states. Regarding notification, states should inform the secretary general of the United Nations to the greatest extent possible of the nature of their DBS activities, and, as to disruption, states shall take all necessary measures in order to prevent disruption between services with due regard to priority of communications relating to the safety of life.

SUMMARY

Although this study used as primary unit of analysis the various statements by the representatives, data on the professional background of the delegation heads as well as size and composition of the groups were collected to provide insights into overall trends in the Working Group on Direct Broadcast Satellites.

Regarding the professional background of the delegation heads, an increase of diplomats from 50 to 73 percent and a correlative decrease in experts (for example, scientists) could be observed (Table 1). An overview of the professional background of the other members of the delegations (for example, alternate representatives, advisors)

TABLE 1

Professional Background of Delegation Heads, 1969-74
(in percent)

	Session				
Profession	First (1969)	Second (1969)	Third (1970)	Fourth (1973)	Fifth (1974)
Diplomat	50	50	72	79	73
Scientist	27	27	16	4	7
Politician/ administrator	18	14	8	13	13
Broadcaster	5	9	4	4	7

Source: Lists of participants in UN documents A/AC.105/49 (1969); A/7621/Add.1 (1969); A/AC.105/83 (1970); A/AC.105/WG/INF.1 (1973); and A/AC.105/WG.3/INF.2 (1974).

TABLE 2

Professional Background of Delegation Members, 1969-74
(in percent)

Profession	Session				
	First (1969)	Second (1969)	Third (1970)	Fourth (1973)	Fifth (1974)
Diplomat	60	51	66	62	64
Scientist	10	12	8	11	7
Politician/ administrator	21	33	11	18	22
Broadcaster	9	4	15	9	7

Source: Lists of participants in UN documents A/AC.105/49 (1969); A/7621/Add.1 (1969); A.AC.105/83 (1970); A/AC.105/WG/INF.1 (1973); and A.AC.105/WG.3/INF.2 (1974).

yielded basically the same trend. The shifts between 1969 and 1974, however, were not as dramatic as in the case of delegation heads; also, the proportion of the politicians/administrators remained relatively high (about 20 percent) throughout the period under investigation (Table 2).

In addition to these changes in the composition of the delegations, the description of the historical events surrounding DBS reveals another constant element: the close cooperation between Canada and Sweden that resulted in joint working papers and draft proposals. The declared purpose of these common efforts has been to mediate between the extreme positions held by the USSR and the United States. While Canada was motivated to occupy this compromise position (described in Chapter 5) by the perception of its national interest in the case of DBS,[163] the Swedish policy was indirectly influenced by its holding the chairmanship of the working group which also demanded a position of compromise in order to secure continued support from the majority of the delegations. As the international legislative process unfolded, the Swedish-Canadian position gained a significance that far transcended this coincidence of national interests. It has become a symbol for the possibility of compromise and moderation of seemingly irreconcilable ideologies. The basic thrust of these two countries' view can be superficially described as for prior consent but against content regulation. This perspective has become an acceptable guideline for numerous neutral and nonaligned states that did not feel the necessity for advancing their own ideas in great detail, be it in the form of a working paper or draft principles. Moreover, some countries at times used a simple affirmative reference to the Canadian-Swedish views as sufficient definition of their own stands.[164]

The intellectual thoroughness of their input, their quasi-academic approach to questions of both communications and international law as well as the wide acceptance of their position supported by the weight of the chairmanship, brought Canada and Sweden a great deal of prestige and influence in the matter of DBS.

The following chapter will proceed to an analysis and systematic examination of the documentary evidence gathered in the historical-descriptive part of the study.

NOTES

1. See also UN Document OSAD/Background Paper no. 1 (WG-3), February 7, 1969, from which are drawn many sources used in this section.

2. "Case Study," p. 44.

3. Statement by Decarvalho Silos (Brazil), UN General Assembly Agenda, Item 28, Annex 21, Document A/5549, add. 1 (1963).

4. UN Document A/RES.1962 (XVII), December 24, 1963.

5. Conference room paper no. 1 of March 23, 1964.

6. Ibid.

7. Ibid. See also, "Case Study," p. 44.

8. UN Document A/AC.105/C.1/WP.26 (1964).

9. UN Document A/AC.105/20 (1964), p. 10.

10. Statement by the delegate of Brazil, UN Document A/AC.105/WG.I:SR.7 (1965), p. 6.

11. "Case Study," p. 45.

12. UN Document A/AC.105/C.2/SR.57 (1966), p. 13.

13. UN Document OSAD/Background Paper no. 1, op. cit., p. 4.

14. UN Document A/AC.105/C.2/WP.No. 19 (1966). (Emphasis added.)

15. UN Document A/AC.105/C.2./SR.68 (1966), pp. 46-61. See also UN Document OSAD/Background Paper, op. cit., pp. 8-12.

16. UN Document OSAD/Background Paper, op. cit., pp. 9-10.

17. "Case Study," p. 46.

18. UN Document A/RES.2222 (XXI), December 19, 1966.

19. General Assembly, 21st Session, First Committee, 1493rd meeting (December 17, 1966).

20. UN Document A/RES.222 (XXI), p. 4(b), December 19, 1966.

21. UN Document A/AC.105/PV.47 (1967), p. 32.

22. Ibid.

23. Ibid., pp. 13, 37, 51-52.

24. UN Document A/AC.105/C.2/SR.80 (1967), p. 15.

25. UN Document A/C.1PV.1501 (1967), p. 17 (Emphasis added.)

26. Ibid.

27. UN Document A/C.1/PV.1499 (1967), pp. 27, 50-57.

28. UN Document A/C.1/PV.1498 (1967), pp. 11-15.

29. General Assembly Resolution 2260 (XXII), 1967.

30. UN Document A/AC.105/C.2/L.49 (1968)

31. UN Document A/AC.105/C.s/SR.104 (1968), p. 9.

32. UN Document A/7285, Annex III (1968), p. 136.

33. UN Document A/AC.105/PV.54 (1968), pp. 31-32.

34. Ibid.

35. UN Document A/AC.105/C.s/SR.104 (1968), p. 136.

36. Statement by the delegate of Sweden, UN Document A/AC. 105/PV.55 (1968), pp. 62-70.

37. Ibid.

38. UN Document A/AC.105/PV.54-58.

39. "Case Study," p. 47.

40. Ibid.

41. UN Document A/7285 (1968), pp. 5-6.

42. Ibid.

43. Ibid.

44. List of participants," in UN Document A/7621/Add. 1 (1969), pp. 13-20.

45. Ibid.

46. In the order listed: UN Documents (1969) A/AC.105/49, A/AC. 105/50, and A/AC.105/52.

47. UN Document A/AC.105/49 (1969), pp. 79-80.

48. UN Document A/AC.105/50 (1969), p. 2.

49. UN Document A/AC.105/52 (1969), pp. 1-3.

50. Ibid., p. 4. (Emphasis added.)

51. UN Document A/7621/Add.1 (1969), p. 31 (Emphasis added.)

52. UN Document A/7621/Add. 1 (1969), p. 10. The costs of the satellites themselves are not included, however, because they were likely to vary greatly. The relatively modest cost of the earth stations transmitting to the satellite has not been included either.

53. "List of participants," in UN Document A/7621/Add.1 (1969), pp. 43-52.

54. Ibid.

55. In the order listed: UN Documents (1969) A/AC.105/WG.3/ WP.1, A/AC.105/63, A.AC.105/59, A/AC.105/61, A.AC.105/62, A/AC.105/64, A.AC.105/65 and A.AC.105/60.

56. UN Document A/AC.105/59 (1969), pp. 8-9.

57. Ibid., pp. 25-26.

58. UN Document A/AC.105/65 (1969), p. 13.

59. Ibid.

60. UN Document A.AC.105/63 (1969), p. 2.

61. Ibid.

62. UN Document A/AC.105/62 (1969), p. 2.

63. Ibid.

64. Ibid., p. 5.

65. Ibid., p. 6.

66. UN Document A.AC.105/61 (1969), pp. 2-3.

67. UN Document A/AC.105/64 (1969), p. 2.

68. UN Document A/AC.105/60 (1969), p. 3.

69. Ibid., pp. 3, 6.

70. UN Document A/7621/Add.1 (1969), p. 40.

71. Ibid., p. 41.

72. Ibid., p. 42.

73. "List of participants," in UN Document A/AC.105/83 (1970), pp. 19-23.

74. Ibid.

75. UN Press Release OS/379 (May 8, 1970), p. 1.

76. In the order listed: UN Documents (1970) A/AC.105/WG.3/L.1, A/AC.105/WG. 3/ORP.1, and A/AC.105/WG.3/CRP.2.

77. UN Document A.AC.105/WG.3/L.1 (1970).

78. UN Press Release OS/382 (May 13, 1970), p. 2.

79. Ibid.

80. UN Document A/AC.105/WG.3/L.1 (1970), pp. 36-39.

81. UN Press Release OS/381 (May 12, 1970), p. 2.

82. Ibid.

83. UN Document A/AC.105/WG.3/CRP.2, reproduced as Annex V in UN Document A/AC.105/83 (1970), pp. 29-31.

84. UN Press Release OS/381 (May 12, 1970), pp. 4-5.

85. Ibid., p. 5.

86. UN Document A/AC.105/83 (1970), Annex V, pp. 29-30.

87. Ibid., pp. 30-31.

88. "Model General Principles for the Use of Artificial Earth Satellites for Radio and Television Broadcasting," UN Document A/AC. 105/WG.3/CRP.1, reproduced as Annex IV in UN Document A/AC. 105/83 (1970), pp. 27-28.

89. UN Document A/AC.105/83, pp. 27-28.

90. UN Press Release OS/380 (May 11, 1970), p. 4.

91. Ibid.

92. In the order listed, Argentina: UN Press Release OS/381 (May 12, 1970), p. 7; Belgium: UN Press Release OS/382 (May 13, 1970), pp. 3-4; Mexico: UN Press Release OS/382 (May 13, 1970), p. 5; Italy: UN Press Release OS/382 (May 13, 1970), p. 5; Brazil: UN Press Release OS/384 (May 19, 1970), p. 3.

93. In the order listed, United States: UN Press Release OS/380 (May 11, 1970), p. 3; Belgium: UN Press Release OS/384 (May 19, 1970), p. 4; United Kingdom: UN Press Release OS/381 (May 12, 1970), p. 4; USSR: UN Press Release OS/384 (May 19, 1970), p. 5; France: UN Press Release OS/384 (May 19, 1970), p. 3; Czechoslovakia: UN Press Release OS/384 (May 19, 1970), p. 3.

94. UN Press Release OS/384 (May 19, 1970), p. 5.

95. Ibid., p. 6.

96. UN Document A/AC.105/83 (1970), p. 15.

97. Ibid., p. 16.

98. Ibid.

99. Ibid.

100. UN Document A/8020 (1970), p. 13.

101. General Assembly Resolution 2733A (XXV) (1970), referred to in UN Document A/8720 (1972), p. 10.

102. UN Document A/AC.105/83 (1970), p. 15.

103. UN Document A/8771 (1972), pp. 1-2.

104. UN Document A/8720 (1972), p. 11.

105. UN Document A/8730 (1972), p. 14. For the full text of Resolution 2916 (XXVII), see Appendix B of this study.

106. UN Press Release UNESCO/2060 (November 15, 1972), p. 1.

107. UN Document A/8771 (1972), p. 1.

108. Ibid.

109. UN Document A/8771 (1972), pp. 1-5. For an elaboration of the USSR proposal see B. G. Dudakov, "Legal Aspects of Direct Tele-vision Broadcasting," Colloquium on the Law of Outer Space 16 (1974): pp. 65-70.

110. Department of State Bulletin 67 (December 11, 1972), p. 29.

111. United Kingdom: UN Document A/C.1/PV.1864 (1972), p. 7; Australia: UN Document A/C. 1/PV.1863 (1972), p. 33.

112. UN Document A/C.1/PV.1864 (1972), pp. 28-30.

113. Ibid., p. 31.

114. UN Document A/C.1/PV.1870 (1972), p. 46. Similar state-ment made by the representative of Mongolia: UN Document A/C.1/PV. 1868 (1972), p. 37.

115. UN Document A/C.1/PV.1867 (1972), p. 47.

116. UN Document A/C.1/PV.1862 (1972), pp. 16-20.

117. UN Document A/C.1/PV.1867 (1972), p. 31.

118. In the order listed: UN Documents (1972) A/C.1/PV.1865 through 1867.

119. UN Document A/C.1/PV.1868 (1972), p. 72.

120. Iran: UN Document A/C.1/PV.1865 (1972), p. 31: Chile: UN Document A/C.1/PV.1867 (1972), p. 57.

121. USSR: UN Document A/C.1/PV.1863 (1972), pp. 23-25; France: UN Document A/C.1/PV.1862 (1972), p. 7.

122. Department of State Bulletin 67 (December 11, 1972), p. 687.

123. In the order listed: UN Documents (1972) A/C.1/PV.1864, p. 6; 1863, p. 32; 1864, p. 28.

124. Mexico: UN Document A/C.1/PV.1867 (1972), p. 31.

125. Egypt: UN Document A/C.1/PV.1866 (1972), p. 48.

126. Department of State Bulletin 67 (December 11, 1972): pp. 687-88.

127. The abstentions were as follows: Central African Republic, Fiji, Gabon, Israel, Lesotho, Nicaragua, Tunisia; UN Monthly Chronicle 9 (December 1972): p. 39.

128. UN Press Release UNESCO/2060 (November 15, 1972).

129. Values in Conflict, p. 37.

130. "List of participants," UN Document A/AC.105/WG/INF.1 (1973).

131. Ibid.

132. In the order listed: UN Documents (1973) A.AC.105/WG.3/L.4, A/AC.105/L.71, and A/8771.

133. UN Document A/AC.105/WG.3/L.4 (1973), pp. 13-14.

134. Article V in ibid., p. 17.

135. Article VI in ibid. For a discussion of the various views on spillover see "Summary of Bellagio Conference," in Values in Conflict, pp. 111-12.

136. Values in Conflict, p. 14.

137. Articles IV and X in UN Document A/AC.105/WG.3/L.4 (1973), and Values in Conflict, pp. 16-18.

138. Values in Conflict, p. 16.

139. "Canada. Transcript of a Statement made by Mr. Erik B. Wang to the Working Group on Direct Broadcast Satellites, United Nations, New York, June 18, 1973," p. 3.

140. "Canadian Delegation to the United Nations. Press Release No. 3 (June 12, 1973)," p. 5.

141. Ibid.

142. UN Document A/AC.105/L.71 (1973), p. 1.

143. Ibid., p. 3.

144. "United States Mission to the United Nations. Press Release USUN-59 (June 15, 1973)," p. 2.

145. Ibid., p. 5.

146. Ibid.

147. Ibid., p. 6.

148. Quoted in ibid. Regarding the First Amendment debate see also "Direct Satellite Broadcasting and the First Amendment," Harvard International Law Journal 15 (Spring 1974): pp. 515-27.

149. UN Press Release USUN-59, pp. 6-7.

150. Ibid., p. 7.

151. Ibid.

152. All statements in the following discussion are drawn from UN Press Releases, OS/555 through 565 (June 13-22, 1973).

153. UN Document A/AC.105/117 (1973).

154. General Assembly Resolution 3182(XXVII).

155. "List of participants," UN Document A/AC.105/WG.3/INF.2 (1974).

156. Ibid.

157. In the order listed: UN Documents (1974) A/AC.105/WG.3/L.8, A/AC.105/WG.3 (V)/CRP.2, and A.AC.105/WG.3 (V)/CRP.3.

158. Edward McWhinney, "The Antinomy of Policy and Function in the Institutionalization of International Telecommunications Broadcasting," Columbia Journal of Transnational Law 13 (1974): p. 20.

159. For a discussion of the U.S. position see Monroe Price, "Summary of Conference Proposals," in Values in Conflict, pp. 99-107.

160. This and the following statements were drawn from UN Press Releases OS/608 and 609 (March 15 and March 20, 1974).

161. UN Document A/AC.105/127 (1974).

162. In this section the author has relied largely on the 1975 draft principles as reproduced in Appendix A; European Broadcasting Union, "Memorandum on Direct Television Broadcasting by Satellite," Geneva, 1974; and personal notes taken during the legal subcommittee meeting of 1975.

163. See for example the statement by the Canadian delegate to the fourth session of the working group on DBS, quoted in "Canada. Transcript of a statement made by Mr. Erik B. Wang to the Working Group on Direct Broadcast Satellites" (New York: United Nations, June 18, 1973): p. 3.

164. See for example the statement of the Austrian delegate to the meeting of the legal subcommittee, February/March 1975, "Legal Sub-Committee. Statement by the Austrian Representative, Mr. Alexander Christiani on the question of Direct Broadcast Satellites on February 25, 1975," mimeographed, (New York: United Nations, 1975) p. 3, which reads in part: ". . . It is no secret that my delegation finds itself in general agreement with the views presented by Sweden and Canada. . . ." This observation and the following paragraph are drawn from personal attendance at the meeting.

4

EVALUATION:
PATTERNS OF THE
REGULATORY PROCESS

Chapter 3 provided a documentation of the increasing concern of the international community with the issue of direct satellite broadcasting as it has manifested itself within the framework of the UN Committee on the Peaceful Uses of Outer Space and its subsidiary bodies. The purpose of the present chapter is to discern the patterns of this involvement in both formal (procedural) and substantive (qualitative) terms and present some general conclusions.

THE INTERNATIONAL LEGISLATIVE PROCESS

Over the years, scholarly attention has focused on the role of the United Nations in the making of international law. At the center of these discussions have been considerations about the legal significance of General Assembly Resolutions.[1] The various factors that determine nations' decision making within the United Nations—especially their voting behavior—have also been investigated from a social science perspective.[2]

Gotlieb and Dalfen in a 1969 study[3] introduced a novel element. They investigated the UN regulatory process itself and applied it to the particular case of the ordering of new (space) technology. With special, but not exclusive, reference to DBS they suggested that these UN efforts could be seen in the light of "the emergence of an embryonic international legislative process," with the UN Outer Space Committee "playing the role of parliamentary standing committees and the (UN General) Assembly that of a parliament—albeit one whose 'acts' must be ratified by the governments of members."[4] The authors went on to say that the committees have "indeed shown their ability to study and pursue important legal questions and the General Assembly has demonstrated its willingness to pass resolutions encouraging legal development." It might be added that the specialized agencies have shown a readiness and "a high degree of competence in preparing briefs and studies . . . and in providing general expertise to the committees, in the manner of effectively operating government departments." In respect to direct satellite broadcasting, the ITU, UNESCO, and the UN Secretariat (Outer Space Affairs Division) have played what amounts to a "departmental" role.[5]

Gotlieb and Dalfen discerned a three-stage pattern.[6] In the first stage, a particular issue would be examined in the appropriate standing committee of the General Assembly. Not infrequently, these committees would establish subcommittees to discuss particular aspects of their subject likely to require ongoing treatment, for example the Legal Subcommittee of the Outer Space Committee and working groups with a more ad hoc mandate, such as the Working Group on Direct Broadcast Satellites. These deliberations would result in reports to the General Assembly.[7]

The second stage comprises substantive Generaly Assembly resolutions on particular subjects, extending in some cases to declarations of principles such as the 1963 declaration of principles to govern outer space activities.[8]

The third stage is characterized by the conclusion of an international convention drafted by the appropriate committee and commended to members by the General Assembly. This had been the case, for example, with the Outer Space Treaty.[9]

The Gotlieb/Dalfen approach attempts to explain UN efforts in the international ordering of new realms, especially outer space, which have been opened for human activity through technological advances. The regulation of direct satellite broadcasting, therefore, falls clearly within the scope of such a model whose three stages —committee work, General Assembly resolutions, and conventions —are easily discernible from the history of UN involvement in this particular area.

The Outer Space Committee and its subcommittees —especially the Working Group on Direct Broadcast Satellites —have been concerned with the study and examination of the issue; its reports have formed the basis for General Assembly resolutions that established guidelines for the general course of future action. At this writing, the process has reached the early phase of its third stage: the drafting of principles that may ultimately lead to the conclusion of an international convention or agreement. The general approach suggested by Gotlieb and Dalfen appears to be supported by the evolution of DBS-related events.

The history of UN concern with DBS as outlined in the previous chapter allows for a refinement of the Gotlieb/Dalfen approach. The present study proposes an approach that is deduced from the course of historical events themselves and distinguishes four stages: (1) issue making, (2) study, (3) reaction to outside events, and (4) drafting of proposals.

First Stage: Issue Making

This first stage is characterized by the gradual perception of DBS as an issue in its own right which, of course, was seen as interwoven into the larger context of the more general question of the peaceful uses of outer space. Initially the subject was only discussed in conjunction with broader issues such as the 1963 declaration of legal principles[10] and the preparatory work for the Outer Space Treaty of 1967. The DBS debate soon developed characteristics and a momentum of its own. By the close of 1967, the General Assembly had officially recognized the "existence" of DBS[11] by referring to it directly.

In structural and processual terms, the interplay between the parent committee and subcommittees on the one hand and the General Assembly on the other began to take shape. Characteristically, the issue of DBS was for the first time raised directly in the scientific and technical subcommittee. The problem was largely seen as a technical one and almost entirely in the hands of "experts."[12] At this time, various attempts by concerned member states to place DES on the agenda of a full committee meeting or UN conferences proved abortive.[13] So did a proposal to include a special DBS paragraph in the Outer Space Treaty of 1967.[14] Nevertheless, these constant reminders—usually presented with a sense of urgency and concern by a variety of delegations for a variety of reasons—contributed to the making of the issue.

It is important to note that the Outer Space Committee and its subsidiary bodies proceed according to the principle of unanimity. Theoretically, a single delegation can veto any majority decision. Stalemates occur frequently. It is usually at this point that the General Assembly, as a source of majority will, will act to determine any further course of the committee work. So it was with DBS on several occasions. While the Outer Space Committee could not reach a consensus either on the degree of urgency surrounding the DES issue or on the nature of the approach (technical versus legal) to be taken, the General Assembly in the previously mentioned Resolution 2260 of 1967 took the initiative by requesting the Outer Space Committee to "study the technical feasibility of communications by direct broadcasts from satellites and the current and foreseeable developments in this field."[15]

The events of 1968, then, produced the completion of the issue-making stage. At first, the legal subcommittee proposed that the question of DBS should be placed on the agenda of the scientific and technical subcommittee.[16] However, when the full committee met in the fall of 1968, the results of the Vienna UN Outer Space Conference of August of the same year had to be taken into account. They suggested that the technology of DBS would be available "in about five years." This was not essentially new information. However, the widespread publicity surrounding official UN conferences rendered it a great deal of political and psychological impact. The Outer Space Committee then,

suggested and the General Assembly adopted a resolution requesting
the committee to set up a special working group on DBS.[17]

The establishment of the Working Group on Direct Broadcast Satellites signified not only the official recognition of the issue but also
its institutionalization with far-reaching implications. Like any domestic bureaucracy, UN institutions show a tendency of maintaining
themselves. They develop their own momentum carried on by the accumulated expertise of a relatively small group of insiders and the
stakes individuals and countries acquire in an effort's success, however defined. Such a highly specialized group as the working group
on DBS has an even stronger drive towards justifying its existence.
Failure to achieve agreements in this area could spell failure of many
efforts. Thus, the very decision of the General Assembly to isolate the
discussions on DBS from those in other subcommittees was indicative
of the international community's recognition of the importance of the
issue but also of its willingness to let the question evolve on its own
pace. This is not in contradiction with the elaborate process of report-
ing and control that exists between the working groups and the parent
committee as well as the General Assembly.

In summary, then, this first stage of the process was characterized
by, inter alia, the following elements: movement from a technical to a
political approach; perceived (imaginary or real, or both) sense of urgency; isolation and institutionalization; interest that transcends narrow circles of specialists—usually generated by a wave of publicity.

Second Stage: Study

This second stage, running from 1969 to 1970, was characterized
by the desire of the international community to find out more about
direct satellite broadcasting and the issues it raised, through studies
of the technical, political, legal, and other aspects of the activity.
During this period the working group issued its first three reports.
The contribution of the first report[18] was to discuss the technical
feasibility of DBS and other technical and economic considerations
pertaining to the activity. The second report[19] provided a broad overview and survey of the key problem areas related to DBS, specifically
in regard to radio frequencies and geostationary orbit positions, to
certain questions of international law, including the Outer Space Treaty,
and to the content of programs that might be broadcast by satellite.

The third meeting[20] marked the end of the study stage. While some
delegations saw a need for further study, others considered the time had
come for the elaboration of legal principles guiding DBS activities. The
conflict between the operational and legislative approach to the ordering of new technology (see the following section) broke wide open and
even the meaning of the 1969 timetable regarding the technical

feasibility of DBS became subject to disputes. No specific agreement
on a further meeting of the working group could be achieved and the
third report could only suggest that the Outer Space Committee consider the reconvening of the working group when further material of
substance was available, mainly as a result of work done in the same
field by UNESCO and ITU.[21]

This latter portion of the study stage is characterized by a waning
influence of the experts. As noted in Chapter 4, while during the first
two sessions of the working group half of the delegations were headed
by specialists (scientists, politicians/administrators, broadcasters)
the third session witnessed a dramatic increase of the generalists
(diplomats).

The high percentage of diplomats in all sessions is caused by
numerous one-person delegations that are almost always headed by a
member of the permanent mission to the United Nations. In the DBS
working group relative increase of diplomats from 50 to 72 percent
and the correlative decrease in specialists are a function of the general movement from a technical to a political (diplomatic) approach. In
this particular case, the pace of the shift itself emerged as point of
controversy which led to a stalemate that expressed itself in a dis-
continuation of the working group for more than two years.

Third Stage: Reaction to Outside Events

This stage ran from 1971 to 1972. By "outside events" this approach
refers to developments outside the Outer Space Committee upon which it
had only limited or indirect influence:

1. The decisions and recommendations adopted by the ITU at the World
   Administrative Radio Conference for Space Telecommunications, in
   Geneva, in 1971, that produced legal definitions of the various
   forms of DBS activities and regulations regarding spillover and
   access to frequency spectrum and geostationary orbit (discussed
   in Chapter 1).
2. The submission of the UNESCO Delcaration of Guiding Principles
   on the Use of Satellite Broadcasting for the Free Flow of Information, the Spread of Education and Greater Cultural Exchange, that,
   albeit not legally binding, covered areas that largely overlap with
   the working group's concerns.[22]
3. The request of the Soviet Union of August 1972 to include in the
   agenda of the 1972 General Assembly the question of the elaboration of an international convention on principles governing the use
   by states of artificial earth satellites for direct television broadcasting.[23]

4. The further advance of satellite broadcasting technology, especially the progress made towards the Indian-American SITE project.[24]

These events generated two decisive actions: First, the Outer Space Committee agreed to reconvene the Working Group on Direct Broadcast Satellites in 1973.[25] Second, the General Assembly adopted Resolution 2916 of November 9, 1972, in which it requested the committee to "undertake as soon as possible the elaboration of principles governing the use by states of artificial earth satellites for direct television broadcasting with a view to concluding an international agreement or agreements."[26]

This reaction stage is marked by a mixture of inactivity and dramatic action. This can be seen in the lack of UN activity leading up to General Assembly Resolution 2916 that went far beyond previous assembly guidance of the Outer Space Committee's DBS involvement. It specifically requested the elaboration of principles and sweepingly brushed aside a minority concern regarding the advisability of such principles in the light of insufficient knowledge about the exact nature of future DBS activities. Undoubtedly, the personal intervention of the foreign minister of the Soviet Union who introduced a complete USSR draft convention on DBS elevated the issue from relative obscurity to the limelight of international diplomacy. This act in turn produced changes in the diplomatic atmosphere that expressed themselves during the November 1972 debate on Resolution 2916. A great deal of publicity was generated and the result of the final vote—102 to 1—virtually catapulted[27] the international legislative process into its fourth—and current—stage.

Fourth Stage: Drafting of Proposals
on Direct Broadcast Satellites

This stage began at the fourth session of the working group in 1973 which saw the discussion of several draft proposals and is at this writing still in the process. During the 1974 session further drafts were introduced and the working group succeeded in conceptually isolating 14 principles. Although still interdisciplinary in nature, the working group increasingly adopted characteristics of a legal drafting group. As to the professional background of the delegation heads, the previously observed trend continued. The percentage of diplomats increased to 79 percent (in 1973), that of scientists declined to 7 percent (in 1974).

In 1973, the General Assembly introduced a shift in venue from the working group to the legal subcommittee.[28] The legal subcommittee met in 1974 and early in 1975 to consider the draft principles. As the working group on DBS has so far not been further reconvened, the issue of DBS has lost the exclusive treatment it enjoyed during 1969-74. In the legal subcommittee, it is but one issue among many (for example, remote sensing, moon treaty, and so on).

The drafting stage, especially as it unfolds in the legal subcommittee, is characterized by a step-by-step procedure of eliminating disagreements over particular principles, paragraphs, words. International lawyers dominate. The process of negotiations, bargaining, and give-and-take resembles traditional drafting efforts at international agreements. As consensus on the desirability of some form of principles has been achieved, disagreements, however wide, on particular paragraphs or even philosophies do not appear as a threat to the overall effort and, in a way, are to be expected. Since the dimension of DBS as a UN issue has been reduced to an agenda item—albeit dealt with on a priority basis—failure to achieve consensus cannot endanger the morale of the parent committee that has sufficiently proved itself in the past through the successful conclusion of such monumental tasks as the Outer Space Treaty of 1967 and other international conventions.

It seems possible that the overall reduction of effort and determination regarding the regulation of DBS, its institutional downgrading as an independent issue in the outer space family—at least for the present— may very well contribute to the creation of a diplomatic climate more favorable to consensus and agreement than there was in the past. One obvious result of the current state is a reduced amount of publicity surrounding the DBS debate. Consequently, the political pressures are diminished and the stakes appear lower which in turn could lead to an atmosphere of compromise and cooperation.

LEGISLATIVE VERSUS OPERATIONAL APPROACH

The previous section organized the sequence of events of the international legislative process involving DBS around a conceptual framework. The present and the following sections will turn to a systematization of two substantive questions relating to member states' positions: (1) what philosophic considerations govern the various nations' general approach to the regulation of the technological innovation of DBS?; (2) when examining the countries' positions on two key issues against the background of a continuum of free flow versus control of information, where do they stand in relation to each other?

The former question, as noted previously, has been viewed in terms of an approach that distinguishes between a legislative orientation that eventually culminates in an international convention and an operational orientation emphasizing international cooperation in establishing and operating actual systems using new technology.[29] This dual approach has been elaborated and refined by Dalfen regarding both DBS and remote earth sensing by satellites.[30] He depicted the legislative approach as involving the positing of norms and rules while the

operational approach was described as advocating their development
on the basis of actual practice. "The former draws on norms and analogies in other areas of international law while the latter focuses on the
activity itself and on its own particular technology."[31]

Dalfen also listed some of the advantages and disadvantages of
each approach. The advantages of the legislative approach "lie in its
explicitness and its ability to record the express interests of states
and the principles on which they are in agreement."[32] Its disadvantages
lie in the " 'a prioristic' nature that can involve responses to nonexistent
problems that may impose unnecessary constraints on the technology."[33]

The advantages of the operational approach "lie in its ability to
circumvent hypothetical problems and to build rules on proven patterns
of workable co-operation"; its disadvantages lie in the fact that "the
countries which are masters of the technology are in an advantageous
position to dictate the terms of co-operation, without fully enough
taking into account the interests of third parties."[34]

McWhinney alluded to basically the same concept—without using
Dalfen's terminology. Siding with the "operational approach," he sees
in a priori legal codes and abstract general principles a danger for
"functionally-developed" and "functions-oriented" international organizations like INTELSAT and ITU by involving them in political-ideological
conflicts.[35] In another context he referred to the "operational approach"
as being "empirical" and "pragmatic."[36]

These two methods of approaching the regulation of technological
innovation emerge with particular clarity from the history of UN concern

TABLE 3

Operational Versus Legislative Approach

Operational	Middle Position	Legislative
United States	Canada	USSR
United Kingdom	Sweden	Czechoslovakia
Belgium	Australia	German Democratic
Japan	Austria	Republic
Italy	Pakistan	Poland
Federal Republic of	India	Brazil
Germany		France
		Mexico
		Egypt

Note: This table does not list all 36 member countries. There
was always a certain number of nations that did not send delegations
to the meetings (for example, Albania never showed up). Many delegations expressed their views, but in the most general form   so that
no inference could be made.

Source: Compiled by the author.

with the ordering of direct satellite broadcasting. In the following an attempt will be made to establish an overview identifying the approximate positions of the Outer Space Committee's member countries. It reflects a combination of a state's current attitude and the cumulative thrust of previous statements. Table 3 lists only countries whose positions have been expressly stated or could be easily inferred from the particular delegation's overall stand on DBS.

The operational approach has appeared in three components: (1) Philosophically, its proponents (especially the United States) based their argument on the postulates of the pragmatic doctine, that experience with new technology should precede its regulation; (2) economically, this view contended that premature regulation of the hypothetically feasible technology could hamper its very development; (3) tactically, it led to a policy of delay, to a conscious deemphasis of actual technical progress made. The United States, for example, constantly insisted that it had no direct-to-home DBS capability under development, on the drawing boards, or intended.[37]

The legislative approach, too, has its roots in philosophical considerations based on the Continental tradition of legal thought and perceived national interest (as opposed to the Anglo-Saxon legal tradition that emphasizes pragmatism and the case). Regulation should precede innovation and guide the course of its development. To neglect this would be like setting in motion "a vehicle without a wheel" and would create a "legal vacuum."[38] The Soviet Union and other Socialist states based this approach on the need to prevent possible abuse of DBS, while such developing countries as Egypt feared a sudden technological breakthrough "that could catch us unaware and unprepared."[39]

The middle position is characterized by the view that the two approaches are not mutually exclusive. Experimentation (operation) and regulation should go hand in hand and do not contradict each other.

Trends and Shifts

Although there were no dramatic changes in the basic philosophies of the key countries during 1969-74, significant shifts nevertheless occurred regarding tactical aspects of the two approaches. For example, up to 1973, the United States rejected any form of regulation of DBS, be it principles or a convention. This position was altered in 1974 when the US delegation did submit draft principles that enunciated its views. Similarly, the Soviet Union modified its position from demanding a full-fledged international convention to joining the majority that opted for principles. Canada and Sweden as well as Australia shifted from advocacy of the operational approach in the early 1970s to the middle position they are occupying at present.

FREE FLOW VERSUS CONTROL OF COMMUNICATION

Another way of organizing the various opinions and positions on DBS in a systematic fashion is to view them in terms of the free flow versus the control-of-communication approach. It has been used repeatedly to measure the amount of restrictions that countries impose upon the international flow of information and ideas.[40]

In a 1974 study, de Sola Pool adapted this model to an examination of the working group's overall position on the issue of DBS.[41] Based on the state of affairs after the 1972 General Assembly debate, he developed a five-stage continuum on which the then 28 members of the working group on DBS were positioned. His stages were (1) countries with a liberal position in international broadcasting; (2) countries for regional or organizational controls; (3) developing countries concerned about cultural imperialism; (4) developing countries with a legalistic approach; and (5) countries strongly legalistic.[42]

Pool's approach is very useful in determining the general DBS position of countries while taking into account their stage of development and legal tradition. However, the political and legislative process has moved beyond Pool's description and entered the drafting stage which allows for a specification of his approach. This can be done by examining the way two concrete issues are being treated in the drafting process. Both issues clearly reflect the overarching free flow versus control problem.

The first question to be examined is, what value do countries place on the principle of free flow of information and ideas as enshrined in Article 19 of the Universal Declaration of Human Rights? The history of DBS as an issue of international debate reveals that the following three categories encompass the range of positions taken by the various states in response to this question.

1. Fully applicable to DBS: The principle of freedom of information is of paramount important for the organization of international conduct, especially regarding modern mass communications. The Universal Declaration of Human Rights constitutes an integral part of international law and is legally binding.[43]
2. Partially applicable: The free flow principle is important, but so is the principle of national sovereignty. A balance has to be struck between the two.
3. Not applicable: The principle of the free flow of communication is merely a political thesis and, as such, cannot be regarded as binding under international law. The sovereign rights of states are of supreme importance.[44]

Table 4 reflects the current positions of the nations represented in the Outer Space Committee as they have revealed themselves during

TABLE 4

How Countries View the Applicability of the
Free Flow Principle

Fully Applicable	Partially Applicable	Not Applicable
Belgium	Argentina	Brazil
Federal Republic of	Australia	Bulgaria
Germany	Austria	Czechoslovakia
Italy	Canada	Egypt
Japan	India	France
United Kingdom	Indonesia	German Democratic
United States	Iran	Republic
	Kenya	Hungary
	Lebanon	Mexico
	Nigeria	Mongolia
	Pakistan	Poland
	Sierra Leone	Romania
	Sweden	USSR

Note: This table only lists member countries of the Outer Space
Committee who were represented at the meetings.
Source: Compiled by the author.

the most recent discussions in the legal subcommittee, February 15 to
March 7, 1975. Although previously made statements were taken into
account, the most definite information on a delegation's attitude was
derived from its position on the second article of the current draft principles[45] which deals with "Applicability of International Law." Whether
a country supported or opposed the inclusion of the Universal Declaration of Human Rights —especially its Article 19—served as a clear in-
dication of its view on this matter.

The composition of the "partially applicable" category was established on the basis of statements made by delegates during the drafting
process. Typically, such widely held views as that of the principles
of freedom of information and national sovereignty not being mutually
exclusive, were regarded as indicating this middle position. This
compromise view has developed around the pragmatic Swedish-Canadian
efforts. It has served as a safe middle position for both smaller industrialized countries and the majority of the developing nations. The
former, because of their domestic communication structure and constitutional provisions, are still committed to the concepts of freedom of
speech and information while at the same time perceiving a need for
protection from unwanted foreign broadcasts; Canada serves as an
example. The developing nations, whether or not domestically committed

to the free flow principle, occupy this compromise position because they
do not wish to prejudice present or future cooperation in the field of
DBS with the technologically advanced (Western) states (the United
States, Japan, the Federal Republic of Germany) that have expressed
strong feelings on this matter; India serves as an example.

As to shifts in positions during 1969–75, the general alteration
of Australia's attitude was also expressed in its stand regarding the
free flow principle. Originally closely associated with the U.S. view,
Australia now occupies the middle position.[46] To a lesser extent,
elements of the same trend could also be observed in the position of
such countries as Canada, Sweden, and Austria.

The second question—perhaps the key issue—refers to the delegations' views of the prior consent principle which appears as the fifth
article of the 1975 draft principles. At the present stage of the legislative process, the question appears to present itself in rather absolute
terms. On the basis of the previous documentation the two main views
can be summarized as follows.

The advocates of the principle of prior consent argue that the principle of sovereignty gives to a state the right freely to select and develop its own political, social, economic, and cultural systems. The
concept of exchange implies that the flow should be bilateral and not
in one direction only. States have uneven opportunities in using the
direct broadcasting technology and this factor strenthened the need
to ensure that activities in this area are conducted on the basis of
prior consent.[47]

The opponents of the prior consent principle base their objections
to a system of prior consent on the argument that it would legitimize
international censorship and stifle technological progress. Some of
them also pointed out that the application of this principle would involve
domestic constitutional problems.[48]

As presently conceived the question does not lend itself to compromise and successful bargaining. Therefore, Table 5 shows only two
positions: for prior consent and against prior consent.

The size of the majority in Table 5 is not necessarily indicative
of its homogeneity. As a matter of fact, it agrees only on the desirability of a prior consent provision, not on its scope. The Soviet Union
and others, for instance, envision a rather restrictive interpretation of
prior consent to be seen in conjunction with their insistence on inclusion
of an enumeration of illegal program content. This, of course, is a far
cry from the relative liberal position of Canada and Sweden that limits
itself to suggesting a system of participation that would give the receiving country a say in the program production.

Also, there is no agreement among the majority as to whether prior
consent is to be required for each individual program or only for categories of programs. Moreover, the practical question of how to admin-
istrate such a provision has not been discussed yet in any concrete
form. While some are of the view that the prior consent principle needs

TABLE 5

Prior Consent: Countries For and Against

For	Against
Argentina	Belgium
Australia	Federal Republic of Germany
Austria	Italy
Brazil	Japan
Bulgaria	United Kingdom
Canada	United States
Czechoslovakia	
Egypt	
France	
German Democratic Republic	
Hungary	
India	
Indonesia	
Iran	
Kenya	
Lebanon	
Mexico	
Mongolia	
Nigeria	
Pakistan	
Poland	
Romania	
Sierra Leone	
Sweden	
USSR	

Source: Compiled by the author.

to be complemented by bilateral or multilateral agreements, others suggest the creation of an international agency to monitor and regulate future DBS activities.

Shifts

Except again for the change of Australia's attitude, no major shifts of substance in the positions occurred during 1969-75. It is important to note that the prior consent concept did not move to the center of the DBS debate until 1972. By this time, however, the basic philosophic approaches to DBS had already been formulated, which prevented a fresh view on this principle. Moreover, as the documentation of Chapter 3 clearly shows, both sides have employed an increasingly ideological rhetoric on this matter which was not conducive to compromise and change.

NOTES

1. D. H. N. Johnson, "The Effect of Resolutions of the General Assembly of the United Nations," British Yearbook of International Law 32 (1955–56): pp. 97–122.

2. See for example Jack Vincent, "An Application of Attribute Theory to General Assembly Voting Patterns and Some Implications," International Organization 26 (Summer 1972): 551–82.

3. "Case Study."

4. Ibid., p. 58 (Emphasis added.)

5. Ibid.

6. The authors' approach was summarized by Dalfen, in "DBS and Remote Sensing Compared," pp. 187–88.

7. Ibid., p. 187.

8. Ibid.

9. "DBS and Remote Sensing Compared," p. 187.

10. UN Document A/RES.1962 (XVII), December 24, 1963.

11. General Assembly Resolution 2260 (XXII), 1967.

12. UN Document A/AC.105/20 (1964), p. 10.

13. UN Document A/AC.105/WG.I: SR.7 (1965), p. 6.

14. UN Document A/AC.105/C.2/WP.No. 19 (1966).

15. General Assembly Resolution 2260 (XXII), 1967.

16. UN Document A/7285, Annex III (1968), p. 136.

17. UN Document G.A.RES.2453 B (XXIII), 1968.

18. UN Document A/AC.105/51 (1969).

19. UN Document A/AC.105/66 (1969).

20. Third report, UN Document A/AC.105/83 (1970).

21. Ibid., p. 15.

22. UN Press Release UNESCO/2060 (November 1972), p. 1.

23. UN Document A/8771 (1972), pp. 1–2.

24. UN Document A/AC.105/114 (1972).

25. UN Document A/8720 (1972), p. 11.

26. UN Document A/8730 (1972), p. 14. For the full text of this resolution see Appendix B.

27. UN Monthly Chronicle 9 (December 1972): 39.

28. General Assembly Resolution 3182 (XXVII), 1973.

29. Christane Verdon and Charles M. Dalfen, "La Cooperation regionale: nouvelle voie ou impasse dans le development du droit des satellites de radiodiffusion directe?," Canadian Yearbook of International Law 8 (1970), pp. 39–60.

30. "DBS and Remote Sensing Compared."

31. Ibid., p. 209.

32. Ibid.

33. Ibid.

34. Ibid., p. 210.

35. Edward McWhinney, "The Antinomy of Policy and Function in the Institutionalization of International Telecommunications Broadcasting," Columbia Journal of Transnational Law 13 (1974): 24.

36. Edward McWhinney, ed., The International Law of Communications, (Leyden: Sijthoff, 1971), p. 14.

37. UN Press Release OS/608 (March 15, 1974).

38. Statements by France, UN Press Release OS/381 (May 12, 1970), pp. 4-5, and Mexico (see Chapter 3).

39. UN Document A/C.1/PV.1866 (1972), p. 48.

40. See for example the "Review of the World Press" established annually by the International Press Institute. For the latest report (taking in events up to November 15, 1974), see IPI Report 24 (January 1975): pp. 1-23.

41. Values in Conflict, p. 41.

42. Ibid.

43. For an elaboration of this view see F. S. Ruddy, "Broadcasting Satellites: An American Perspective," Lawyer of the Americas 3 (October 1974): 499-506.

44. For an elaboration of this position see Yuri Kolosov, "TV and International Law," New Times 15 (Moscow: Spring 1974): 14.

45. For the full text of the 1975 draft principles see Appendix A. Information about the countries' stands was gathered from personal observation and interviews, New York, February/March 1975.

46. The shift was announced during the fourth session of the working group on DBS 1973; see UN Press Releases OS/555 through 565 (June 13-June 22, 1973).

47. See also New Delhi Conference, p. 10.

48. This latter view is also shared by the American television networks. See for example Frank Stanton's (CBS) contention that a prior consent provision "would make censorship a principle of international law"; quoted in Tom Grauberg and Kaarle Nordenstreng, "Approaching International Control of Satellite Communication," Instant Research on Peace and Violence 3, no. 1 (1973): 7.

The evolution of the issue of direct satellite broadcasting illustrates significant changes in the nature of the debate on questions of international communications since 1970. These changes are but reflections of larger alterations in the overall distribution of power—especially as evidenced within the UN system, in the economic world order, and in the way traditional identities of national interests dissolve and new ones emerge. It would be a truly monumental task—and far beyond the scope of this study—to detect and describe what exactly constitutes the difference between the years 1970 and 1975 on a global scale.

For the purposes of these general conclusions, it seems appropriate to allude to a few of these changes that have had a direct bearing on the way the international discourse on DBS has been conducted and the actions they generated.

One change refers to the international perception of new communications technology. The technical concern with feasibility came to be replaced by the political concern with control. A study of the reactions of the international community to the new technology of DBS clearly reveals this fact.[1] It was not excitement about a technological breakthrough that has shaped the international discourse; rather it has been concern about possible abuse. While DBS's great potential for spreading education and promoting understanding among peoples has been acknowledged,[2] the atmosphere of the debate has nevertheless been determined by expressions of apprehension and suspicion about space monopoly and cultural invasion (for examples see Chapter 3). Questions of access and control occupy a central position. It is in this context that the conflict between the operational and the legislative approach to the regulation of DBS should be seen. While differences in legal tradition account for some of this conflict, its political relevance is derived from the desire of the majority of countries to have an input into the decisions regarding the development of new technology which may affect them.

Another change is the rise of the so-called Third World which represents a numerical majority in the UN General Assembly—the celebrated "New Majority."[3] These developing nations of Africa, Asia, and Latin America have found themselves increasingly in agreement with each other on a variety of issues. Again, the case of DBS provides a clear illustration of these new realities. From the beginning, the developing countries have voiced similar opinions on DBS. Being increasingly aware of the fact that DBS's very potential will manifest itself first and above all in its application in the developing areas,[4] these countries are nevertheless reluctant to accept this new technology without securing some form of control over its application. The political values they attach to such concepts as cultural integrity and national identity take precedence over the more pragmatic values of efficiency and cost saving that are associated with a less restrictive approach to the application of new technology (for example, DBS).

As for the present, the Soviet Union appears to comprehend the sensitivities of the Third World much better than the United States. The USSR has managed to very skillfully identify its own concerns (which are of a political nature) with those of the Third World which are economic and cultural.[5] The legislative tool to achieve this consensus is the prior consent principle that—at least in its present form— seems to meet both concerns.

A third change has occurred in the context of the international perception of the principle of the free flow of information and ideas as enshrined in the Universal Declaration of Human Rights of 1948. An overview of the statements made on the issue of DBS clearly reveals that the absolutist[6] interpretations of this principle can no longer muster a majority of the international community. While the Soviet Union and other Socialist states have opposed the international applicability of the free flow principle all along, it came to be increasingly called into question by most of the developing countries as well as by some Western nations. The latter view contends that this principle tends to legitimize the presently existing imbalance in the flow of information from a few industrial nations to the developing countries in a one-way fashion. A 1974 UNESCO study, for instance, revealed that nearly 90 percent of all television program exports emanate from only four countries: the United States (150,000 hours per year), the United Kingdom (30,000), France (20,000), and the Federal Republic of Germany (6,000).[7] In order to fill this rather abstract and formal concept with meaning, the widespread argument goes, a certain measure of balance (two-way flow) needs to be established.

In summary, then, modifications in the international perception of new (communication) technology and the principle of the free flow of information as well as the rise of the Third World nations have been contributing factors that influenced the international discourse and action involving direct satellite broadcasting. Both discourse and action found their concrete form in an emerging international regulatory process within the UN Committee on the Peaceful Uses of Outer Space. The very fact that this process was engaged in the case of DBS constitutes a novel element in international communications.

In the past, the international community has entrusted the dealings with problems of the transborder transfer of communications to its specialized agencies such as ITU and UNESCO or it has attempted to create general guidelines for international conduct such as the Universal Declaration of Human Rights or General Assembly resolutions condemning international propaganda.[8]

In the case of DBS, however, the international community felt that the United Nations itself should become involved. Thus, while the specialized agencies, namely ITU and UNESCO, continued to play an important role,[9] the center of action and discussion has moved to the main body of the UN system. This signifies the importance that the international community has attached to the issue of DBS. It is largely a result of the fact that DBS combines elements of two novel, only partly explored, technologies: space and communication.

With respect to questions of outer space there was a general consensus that the United Nations should involve itself in the regulation of international conduct in this new area. Within a few years after Sputnik I, the basic principles governing man's behavior in outer space were drawn up (see Chapter 2, noting the unanimous acceptance of the Outer Space Treaty of 1967). Thus, when the issue of DBS emerged, the international community could build upon a body of already existing norms (Outer Space Treaty) and structures (Outer Space Committee) which have shaped the evolving international legislative process.

DBS, however, is not only a space activity but also an activity involving international communication—in principle, if not in scope similar to traditional international shortwave broadcasting with which the international community has been living for more than half a century. The vast body of experience that has been accumulated, however, has not led to universally agreed-upon principles of conduct.

Regulatory efforts in the field of DBS, then, face a fundamental dilemma. The perception of DBS as space activity is based on widely agreed-upon principles—with no experience. The concept of DBS as communication activity is based on vast experience that produced no agreement.

This dilemma accounts for some of the difficulties that have surrounded the DBS debate. Most nations tend to ground their position on DBS on their previous experience with conventional forms of international communication.[10] DBS as a technological innovation, however, by definition escapes experience and ultimate predictability. Traditional forms of satellite communications (for example, INTELSAT) can furnish only limited guidance as the crucial issue of prior consent is not raised. The absence of experience and predictability, then, forces a recourse to conventional concepts of international communication with the result that past disagreement is projected into the future.

What is needed is a fresh look at DBS as essentially a space activity which, of course, requires a willingness on all parts to take risks especially domestically as bureaucratic consensus is based, above all, on predictability and proof. The early development of principles governing the use of outer space has shown that the international community is willing and capable to act creatively in this new area of human endeavor. A debate on DBS as space activity would move away from such concepts as free flow, censorship, state sovereignty, and so on, that are largely rooted in traditional philosophies of communication and legal tradition. The new debate would draw its concepts from the nature and the potential of the activity itself: access, developmental needs, and the rights of mankind.

NOTES

1. Compare, for example, UN Document A/AC.105/49 (1969) with UN Document A/AC.105/WG.3/L.8 (1974).

2. See Article VII of the U.S. proposal [UN Document A/AC.105/WG.3(v)/CRP.2], and Article III of the USSR draft [UN Document A/AC.105/WG.3(v)/CRP.2].

3. Michael Reisman, "Living With the Majority," The Nation, February 1, 1975, pp. 102-04.

4. Abram Chayes and Paul Laskin, "Report of the Panel on International Telecommunications Policy," in American Society of International Law, Direct Broadcasting from Satellites, (Washington, D.C.: West, 1975), p. 5.

5. Article IV of the Soviet draft principles, for example, considers as "illegal" programs that "undermine the foundations of the local civilizations, culture, way of life, traditions or language," [UN Document A/AC.105/WG.3(v)/CRP.1].

6. For the best illustration of this position, see the US statement to the fourth session of the Working Group on DBS (1973), "United States Mission to the United Nations. Press Release USUN-59 (June 15, 1973)."

7. Kaarle Nordenstreng and Tapio Varis, Television Traffic—A One-Way Street? (Paris: UNESCO, 1974), p. 30.

8. For example, General Assembly Resolution 110 (II), of November 3, 1947.

9. International Telecommunication Union, Final Acts (Genoa: World Administrative Radio Conference for Space Telecommunications, 1971); and UNESO "Guiding Principles," UN Press Release UNESCO/2060, November 15, 1972.

10. See for example the statement of the representative of Belgium that explicitly referred to the benefits this country derives from external broadcasts, UN Document A/C.1/PV.1862 (1972), p. 31.

REPORT OF THE LEGAL SUBCOMMITTEE ON THE WORK OF ITS
FOURTEENTH SESSION (FEBRUARY 10-MARCH 7, 1975)

Report of the Chairman of Working Group II*

1. Following the procedure adopted at its thirteenth session, the
Legal Sub-Committee, on 10 February 1975, established Working Group
II for the item "Elaboration of principles governing the use by States
of artificial earth satellites for direct television broadcasting."
2. At its first meeting held on 25 February, the Working Group decided that it would attempt to deal with all the principles reflected in
the Report of the Working Group on Direct Broadcasting Satellites on
the work of its fifth session (A/AC.105/127), including the five principles considered at the thirteenth session of the Legal Sub-Committee.
3. The Working Group also decided at its first meeting on 25 February to transform itself into a Drafting Group of the whole. The Drafting Group held 10 meetings. The first six meetings were devoted to
the consideration of the principles not discussed at the thirteenth
session of the Legal Sub-Committee and the next two meetings to the
consideration of the five principles which had been discussed previously. The final two meetings were devoted to the finalization of the drafts
to be included in the report of the Working Group.
4. At its meeting on 4 March, the Working Group endorsed the work
of the Drafting Group and decided to request the Sub-Committee to re-
produce the present report, together with the texts of the principles
given below (which include words or sentences in brackets, or alternative formulations, on matters where consensus could not be reached)
as an annex to the report of the Sub-Committee on the work of its
fourteenth session.

Purposes and Objectives

Alternative A

Activities in the field of direct television broadcasting by satellite
should serve the purpose of maintaining international peace and security,

---

*Taken from United Nations General Assembly, Committee on the
Peaceful Uses of Outer Space, UN Document A/AC.105/147 (March
11, 1975), Annex II, pp. 1-6.

developing mutual understanding and strengthening friendly relations and cooperation among all States and peoples, assisting in the social and economic development particularly in the developing countries, facilitating and expanding the international exchange of information, promoting exchanges in the field of culture, science ane economy and enhancing the educational level of peoples of various countries. To this end activities in the field of direct television broadcasting by satellite shall be carried out by States exclusively in a manner compatible with the above-mentioned objectives and with due regard to the provisions of the principle . . . [which relates to the applicability of international law].

Alternative B

Activities in the field of [international] direct television broadcasting by satellite should facilitate and expand the mutual international exchange of information and ideas, promote cultural and scientific exchanges, and enhance the educational level of all peoples. Such broadcasting should encourage the development of mutual understanding, friendly relations, and co-operation among all states and peoples, and should be conducted in a manner compatible with the maintenance of international peace and security. Efforts should be made where appropriate to encourage beneficial applications of direct television broadcasting by satellite which may assist in social and economic development particularly in the developing countries.

Applicability of International Law

[States shall ensure that] Activities in the field of direct television broadcasting by means of artificial earth satellites [are] [should be] conducted in accordance with generally recognized rules of international law including the Charter of the United Nations, the Treaty on Principles Governing the Activities of States in the Exploration and Use of Outer Space, including the Moon and other Celestial Bodies of 27 January 1967, the relevant provisions of the International Telecommunication Convention and its Radio Regulations and in accordance with the principles of international law relating to friendly relations and co-operation among States and human rights [including those contained in the Declaration on Principles of International Law concerning Friendly Relations and Co-operation among States and the Universal Declaration of Human Rights] [and the International Covenant on Civil and Political Rights.]

Rights and Benefits [of States]

Every State has an equal right to conduct and to authorize [under its supervision] activities in the field of direct television broadcasting by means of artificial earth satellites. All States and peoples [and individuals] [are entitled to] [should have an appropriate opportunity for] [should enjoy] equitable sharing without discrimination in the benefits derived from such activities on mutually agreed terms including, subject to national legislation, access to the use of this technology.

International Co-operation

Activities in the field of direct television broadcasting by means of artificial earth satellites [shall be based on] [should encourage] international co-operation. Such co-operation shall be the subject of appropriate arrangements between the States concerned and/or entities authorized by them.

State Responsibility

States shall bear international responsibility for activities in the field of direct television broadcasting by means of artificial earth satellites carried out by them or under their jurisdiction and for the conformity with these principles of any such activities.

When direct television broadcasting by means of artificial earth satellites is carried out by an international organization, responsibility for compliance with these principles shall be borne both by the international organization and by States participating in such organization.

Consent and Participation

Alternative A

Direct television broadcasting by means of artificial earth satellites specifically aimed at a foreign State shall require the consent of that State. The consenting State shall have the right to participate in activities which involve coverage of territory under its jurisdiction. This participation shall be governed by appropriate arrangements between the States involved.

The consent and participation referred to in Principle . . . shall not apply where coverage of the territory of a foreign State results

from radiation of the satellite signal within the limits considered technically unavoidable under the Radio Regulations of the International
Telecommunication Union.

Alternative B

Direct television broadcasting by satellite should be conducted
in accordance with the principles set out herein, and in particular
in accordance with principle. . . . [which relates to participation and
cooperation].It may be subject to such restrictions imposed by the State
carrying out or authorizing it as are compatible with the generally accepted rules of international law relating to freedom of expression, which
includes freedom to seek, receive and impart information and ideas of
all kinds, regardless of frontiers.
The consent of any State in which such broadcasting is received
is not required, but the State carrying it out or authorizing it should
consult fully with any such receiving State which so requests concerning
any restrictions to be imposed by the former State.
The foregoing is without prejudice to the restrictions which may be
imposed in accordance with international law on technical grounds.

Spill-over

Alternative A

In carrying out activities in the field of direct television broadcasting by satellites, all technical means available shall be used to reduce,
to the maximum extent practicable, the radiation over the territory of
other countries [which enable reception of television programmes with
conventional or augmented television sets] unless an agreement has
been previously reached with such countries.

Alternative B

Without prejudice to the ITU regulations concerning the avoidance
of interference, all reasonable means should be used to reduce to the
minimum any unintended radiation of the territory of other countries.

Program Content

[States or their broadcasting entities which participate in direct
television broadcasting by satellite with other States should co-operate
with one another in respect of programming, programme content, production and interchange of programmes.]

[The broadcasting of commercial advertising, direct or indirect
to countries other than the country of origin, should be on the basis
of appropriate agreements between the countries concerned.]

[Notwithstanding the foregoing States undertaking activities in
direct television broadcasting by satellites should in all cases exclude
from the television programs any material which is detrimental to the
maintenance of international peace and security, which publicizes
ideas of war, militarism, national and racial hatred and enmity between
peoples, which is aimed at interfering in the domestic affairs of other
States or which undermines the foundations of the local civilization,
culture, way of life, traditions or language.]

Unlawful/Inadmissible Broadcasts

[States shall regard as unlawful and as giving rise to the international liability of States direct television broadcasts specifically
aimed at a foregin State but carried out without the express consent
of the latter, containing material which according to these principles
should be excluded from programmes, or received as a result of uninten-
tional radiation of the broadcasting State has refused to hold appropriate
consultations with the State in which the broadcasts are received.]

[In case of the transmission to any State of television broadcasts
which are unlawful, that State may take in respect of such broadcasts
measures which are recognized as legal under international law.]

[States agree to give every assistance in stopping unlawful direct
television broadcasting by satellite.]

[Any broadcasts that a State does not wish to be made in its territory or among its population and in respect of which it has made
known such decision to the broadcasting State are inadmissible.]

[Every transmitter, State, international organization or authorized
agency shall refrain from making such broadcasts or shall immediately
discontinue such broadcasts if it has begun to transmit them.]

Duty and Right to Consult

Alternative A

If a State, notwithstanding the provisions of principles . . . and
. . . [Alternative A under "Consent and participation"] and the coordination procedures required under the provisions of the Radio Regulation of the International Telecommunication Union, has reason to
believe that as a result of activities carried out or authorized by other
States in the field of direct television broadcasting by means of satellites, it will be prejudicially affected by radiation over its territory,

it may request that consultations be held. A State receiving such a request shall enter into such consultations without delay.

Alternative B

Any State requested to do so by another State should without delay enter into consultations with the latter State concerning any matter arising from activities in the field of direct television broadcasting carried out or authorized by either of them which are likely to affect the other.

Peaceful Settlement of Disputes

Any disputes that may arise from activities in the field of direct television broadcasting by means of artificial earth satellites should be resolved by prompt consultations among the parties to such disputes. Where a mutually acceptable resolution cannot be achieved by such consultations, it should be sought through other established procedures for the peaceful settlement of disputes.

Copyright, Neighbouring Rights and Protection of Television Signals

[Copyright and neighbouring rights shall not be affected by the use of direct broadcast television.] States shall co-operate on a bilateral and multilateral basis for protection of copyright and neighbouring rights by means of appropriate agreements between the interested States. In such co-operation they shall give special consideration to the interests of developing countries in the use of direct television broadcasting for the purpose of accelerating their national development.
[The provision of the Convention relating to the distribution of programmes carrying signals transmitted by satellite, Brusseles, 1974, shall not be affected by this principle.]

Notification to the United Nations System

In order to promote international co-operation in the peaceful exploration and use of outer space, States conducting or authorizing activities in the field of direct television broadcasting by satellites should inform the Secretary-General of the United Nations to the greatest extent possible of the nature of such activities [including information on the contents of programs]. On receiving the said information, the Secretary-General of the United Nations should disseminate it immediately and effectively to the relevant United Nations specialized agencies, as well as to the public and the international scientific community.

Disruption

In using direct television broadcasting by means of satellites, States shall take all necessary measures in order to prevent disruption between services with due regard to priority of communications relating to the safety of life.

GENERAL ASSEMBLY RESOLUTION 2916, 1972*

Preparation of an international convention on principles governing the use by States of artificial earth satellites for direct television broadcasting.

The General Assembly

Recalling its resolution 2222 (XXI) of 19 December 1966, in which it stressed the importance of international cooperation in the field of activities in the peaceful exploration and use of outer space and the importance of developing the rule of law in this new area of human endeavour,

Recalling further its resolution 2453 B (XXIII) of 20 December 1968, in which it stated that the benefits of space exploration can be extended to States at all stages of economic and scientific development,

Reaffirming the common interest of all mankind in furthering the peaceful exploration and use of outer space for the benefit of all States and for the development of friendly relations and mutual understanding among them,

Bearing in mind that direct television broadcasting should help to draw the peoples of the world together, to widen the exchange of inform- ation and cultural values and to enhance the educational level of people in various countries,

Considering at the same time that direct television broadcasting by means of satellites should take place under conditions in which this new form of space technology will serve only the lofty goals of peace and friendship among peoples,

Mindful of the need to prevent the conversion of direct television broadcasting into a source of international conflict and of aggravation of the relations among States and to protect the sovereignty of States from any external interference,

Noting that the draft convention on principles governing the use by States of artificial earth satellites for direct television broadcasting, submitted to the General Assembly by the Union of Soviet Socialist Republics,

---

*Draft resolution I, A/8864, as amended in plenary; adopted by the assembly on November 9, 1972, by a vote of 102 to 1 (United States), with 7 abstentions.

Desiring to further the elaboration of specific rules of international law governing the activities of States in this field on the basis of the Charter of the United Nations, the Treaty on Principles Governing the Activities of States in the Exploration and Use of Outer Space, including the Moon and other Celestial Bodies and the Declaration on Principles on International Law concerning Friendly Relations and Co-operation among States in accordance with the Charter of the United Nations,

Believing that the activity of States in the field of direct television broadcasting must be based on the principles of mutual respect for sovereignty, non-interference in domestic affairs, equality, co-operation and mutual benefit,

Considering at the same time that the introduction of direct television broadcasting by means of satellites could raise significant problems connected with the need to ensure the free flow of communications on a basis of strict respect for the sovereign rights of States,

1. Considers it necessary to elaborate principles governing the use by States of artificial earth satellites for direct television broadcasting with a view to concluding an international agreement or agreements;

2. Requests the Committee on the Peaceful Uses of Outer Space to undertake the elaboration of such principles as soon as possible;

3. Requests the Secretary-General to transmit to the Committee on the Peaceful Uses of Outer Space all documentation relating to the discussion, at the twenty-seventh session of the General Assembly, of the item entitled "Preparation of an international convention on principles governing the use by States of artificial earth satellites for direct television broadcasting."

BOOKS

Alexandrowicz, Charles Henry. The Law of Global Communications. New York: Columbia University Press, 1971.

Aspen Institute Program on Communications and Society. Control of the Direct Broadcast Satellite: Values in Conflict. Palo Alto: Aspen Institute Program on Communications and Society, 1974.

Berrada, Abderrazak. Frequencies for Broadcasting Satellites. London: International Broadcast Institute, 1972.

Centre National d'Etudes Spatiales. Les Satellites d'Education—Educational Satellites. Paris: Centre National d'Etudes Spatiales, 1971.

Centre National de la Recherche Scientifique. Les Telecommunications par Satellites. Paris: Aspects Juridiques. Paris: Editions Cujas, 1968.

Chayes, Abram. Satellite Broadcasting. London: Oxford University Press, 1973.

Cherry, Colin. World Communication: Threat or Promise? London: Wiley-Interscience, 1971.

Chitnis, E. V. Satellite Instructional Television Experiment (Site). Ahmedeaba: Indian Space Research Organization, 1970.

Comsat. 1974 Report to the President and the Congress. Washington, D.C.: Comsat, 1974.

Ellul, Jacques. Propaganda. New York: Vintage Books, 1965.

Fawcett, J. E. S., ed. International Organization. London: Oxford University Press, 1974.

Gal, Guyla. Space Law. Leyden: A. W. Sijthoff, 1969.

Galloway, Jonathan F. The Politics and Technology of Satellite Communications. Lexington, Mass.: Lexington Books, 1972.

Gerbner, George, et al., eds. Communications Technology and Social
    Policy. New York: John Wiley and Sons, 1973.

Haley, Andrew G. Space Law and Government. New York: Appleton-
    Century-Crafts, 1963.

Han, Henry. International Legislation by the United Nations. New
    York: Exposition-University-Book, 1971.

Havinghurst, Clark C. International Control of Propaganda. Dobbs
    Ferry, N.Y.: Oceana Publications, 1967.

International Telecommunication Union (ITU). Final Acts of the World
    Administrative Radio Conference for Space Telecommunications.
    Geneva: ITU, 1971.

_____. ITU and Space Radiocommunication. Geneva: ITU, 1968.

_____. Eighth Report by the International Telecommunication Union
    on Telecommunication and the Peaceful Uses of Outer Space.
    Geneva: ITU, 1969.

_____. Symposium "Space and Radiocommunication." Geneva:
    ITU, 1969.

_____. Ninth Report by the International Telecommunication Union
    on Telecommunication and the Peaceful Uses of Outer Space.
    Geneva: ITU, 1970.

_____. Tenth Report by the International Telecommunication Union
    on Telecommunication and the Peaceful Uses of Outer Space.
    Geneva: ITU, 1971.

_____. Eleventh Report by the International Telecommunication Union
    on Telecommunication and the Peaceful Uses of Outer Space.
    Geneva: ITU, 1972.

_____. Twelfth Report by the International Telecommunication Union
    on Telecommunication and the Peaceful Uses of Outer Space.
    Geneva: ITU, 1973.

_____. Thirteenth Report by the International Telecommunication
    Union on Telecommunication and the Peaceful Uses of Outer
    Space. Geneva: ITU, 1974.

Kildow, Judith Tegger. INTELSAT: Policy-Maker's Dilemma. Lexington,
    Mass.: Lexington Books, 1973.

Lay, Houston S., and Taubenfeld, Howard. The Law Relating to Activities of Man in Space. Chicago: The University of Chicago Press, 1970.

Leive, David M. International Telecommunications and International Law: The Regulation of the Radio Spectrum. Leyden: A. W. Sijthoff.

McWhinney, Edward, ed. The International Law of Telecommunications. Leyden: A. W. Sijthoff, 1971.

Marcoff, Marco G. Traite de Droit International Public de l'Espace. Fribourg: Editions Universitaires, 1973.

Martin, Charles-Noel. Les Satellites Artificiels. Paris: Presses Universitaires de France, 1965.

Morenoff. Jerome. World Peace Through Space Law. Charlottesville, Va.: The Michie Company, 1967.

Mueller, George Edwin. Communication Satellites. New York: Wiley, 1964.

Murty, B. S. Propaganda and World Public Order. New Haven: Yale University Press, 1968.

Mordenstreng, Kaarle, and Tapio Varis. Television Traffic. A One Way Street? Paris: UNESCO, 1974.

Pool, Ithiel de Sola. "Direct Broadcasting Satellites and the Integrity of National Cultures." In Control of the Direct Broadcast Satellite. Values in Conflict. Palo Alto: Aspen Institute, 1974.

Pool, Ithiel de Sola, et al., eds. Handbook of Communication. Chicago: Rand McNally, 1973.

Prosser, Michael H., ed. Intercommunication Among Peoples. New York: Harper & Row, 1973.

Rydbeck, Olof, and Edward W. Ploman. Broadcasting in the Space Age. Geneva: European Broadcasting Union, 1969.

Salvatore, Giorgio. Communicationes por Satelite. Buenos Aires: Comision Nacional de Investigaciones Espaciales, 1966.

Schiller, Herbert I. The Mind Managers. Boston: Beacon Press, 1973.

Schramm, Wilbur. Communication Satellites for Education, Science and Culture. Paris: UNESCO, 1968.

_____. _Mass Media, and National Development_. Paris: UNESCO, 1964.

Schulze, Brich. _Protection Against Satellites_. Berlin: Franz Vahlen GmbH, 1970.

Sheikh, Ahmed. _International Law and National Behavior_. New York: John Wiley & Sons, 1974.

Smith, Delbert. _International Telecommunication Control_. Leyden: A. W. Sijthoff, 1969.

The Twentieth Century Fund. _Global Communications in the Space Age_. New York: The Twentieth Century Fund, 1972.

UNESCO. _Broadcasting from Space_. Paris: 1970.

_____. _Communication in the Space Age: The Use of Satellites by the Mass Media_. Paris: UNESCO, 1968.

_____. _A Guide to Satellite Communication_. Paris: UNESCO, 1972.

Wells, Alan. _Picture-Tube Imperialism_? New York: Orbis Books, Maryknoll, 1972.

UNITED NATIONS DOCUMENTS

First Committee of the General Assembly

Twenty-fifth Session. _International Co-operation in the Peaceful Uses of Outer Space_. Report of the First Committee (A/8250) New York, 1970.

Twenty-sixth Session. _International Cooperation and the Peaceful Uses of Outer Space_. Report of the First Committee (A/8528). New York, 1971.

Twenty-sixth Session. "_Budget Estimates for the Financial Year 1972._" _International Co-operation in the Peaceful Uses of Outer Space: Report of the Committee on the Peaceful Uses of Outer Space_ (A/C5/1402). New York, 1971.

Twenty-seventh Session. _Preparation of an International Convention on Principles Governing the Use by States of Artificial Earth_

Satellites for Direct Television Broadcasting (A/8864). New York,
1972.

Twenty-eighth Session. Preparation of an International Convention on
Principles Governing the Uses by States of Artificial Earth Satellites
for Direct Television Broadcasting (A/C.1/L.669/Rev. 1). New
York, 1973.

                    Resolutions of the General Assembly

"Resolution 110 (II). Measures to be Taken Against Propaganda and
the Inviters of a New War. 108th Plenary Meeting, 3 November
1947." In Resolutions, Sept.-Nov. 1947, Official Records of the
General Assembly: Second Session (A/519) New York, 1948.

"Resolution 1721 D (XVI). International Co-operation in the Peaceful
Uses of Outer Space. 1085th Plenary Meeting, 20 December
1961." In Resolutions, Sept.-Feb. 1962 Official Records of the
General Assembly: Sixteenth Session, Supplement no. 17 (A/5100),
New York, 1962.

"Resolution 1962 (XVIII). Declaration of Legal Principles Governing
the Activities of States in the Exploration and Use of Outer Space.
1280th Plenary Meeting, 13 December 1963." In Resolutions,
Sept.-Dec. 1963, Official Records of the General Assembly:
Eighteenth Session, Supplement no. 15 (A/5515), New York, 1964.

"Resolution 1963 (XVIII). International Co-operation in the Peaceful
Uses of Outer Space. 1280th Plenary Meeting, 13 December 1963."
In Resolutions, Sept.-Dec. 1963 Official Records of the General
Assembly: Eighteenth Session, Supplement no. 15 (A/5515), New
York, 1964.

"Resolution 2222 (XXI). Treaty on Principles Governing the Activities
of States in the Exploration and Use of Outer Space, Including
the Moon and Other Celestial Bodies. 1499th Plenary Meeting,
19 December 1966." In Resolutions, Sept.-Dec. 1966, Official
Records of the General Assembly: Twenty-first Session, Supplement
no. 16 (A/6316), New York, 1967.

"Resolution 2453 B (XXIII). International Co-operation in the Peaceful
Uses of Outer Space. 1750th Plenary Meeting, 20 December 1968."
In Resolutions, Sept.-Dec. 1968, Official Records of the General
Assembly: Twenty-third Session, Supplement no. 18 (A/7218),
New York, 1969.

"Resolution 2601 (XXIV). International Co-operation in the Peaceful
    Uses of Outer Space. 1836th Plenary Meeting, 16 December 1969."
    In Resolutions, Sept.-Dec. 1969, Official Records of the General
    Assembly: Twenty-fourth Session, Supplement no. 30 (A/7630),
    New York, 1970.

"Resolution 2733 A (XXV). International Co-operation in the Peaceful
    Uses of Outer Space. 1932nd Plenary Meeting, 16 December 1970."
    In Resolutions, Sept.-Dec. 1970, Official Records of the General
    Assembly: Twenty-fifth Session, Supplement No. 28 (A/8028) New
    York, 1971.

"Resolution 2776 (XXVI). International Co-operation in the Peaceful
    Uses of Outer Space. 1998th Plenary Meeting, 29 November 1971."
    In Resolutions, Sept.-Dec. 1971, Official Records of the General
    Assembly: Twenty-sixth Session, Supplement no. 29 (A/8429),
    New York, 1972.

"Resolution 2915 (XXVII). International Co-operation in the Peaceful
    Uses of Outer Space. 2081st Plenary Meeting, 9 November 1972."
    In Resolutions, Sept.-Dec. 1972, Official Records of the General
    Assembly: Twenty-seventh Session, Supplement no. 30 (A/8730),
    New York, 1973.

"Resolution 2916 (XXVII). Preparation of an International Convention on
    Principles Governing the Use by States of Artificial Earth Satel-
    lites for Direct Television Broadcasting. 2081st Plenary Meeting,
    9 November 1972." In Resolutions, Sept.-Dec. 1972, Official
    Records of the General Assembly: Twenty-seventh Session, Sup-
    plement no. 30 (A/8730), New York, 1973.

"Resolution 2917 (XXVII). Preparation of International Instruments or
    United Nations Arrangements on Principles Governing the Use by
    States of Artificial Earth Satellites for Direct Television Broad-
    casting. 2081st Plenary Meeting, 9 November 1972." In Resolu-
    tions, Sept.-Dec. 1972, Official Records of the General Assembly:
    Twenty-seventh Session, Supplement no. 30 (A/8730), New York,
    1973.

"Resolution 3182 (XXVIII). International Co-operation in the Peaceful
    Uses of Outer Space. 2205th Plenary Meeting, 18 December 1973."
    In Resolutions, Sept.-Dec. 1973, Official Records of the General
    Assembly: Twenty-eighth Session, Supplement No. 30, (A/9030),
    New York, 1974.

Committee on the Peaceful Uses of Outer Space

Progress Report on Interim Arrangements for a Global Commercial Com-
    munications Satellite System. Letter dated 27 October 1964 from
    the Deputy Permanent Representative of the United States of America
    to the Secretary-General (A/AC.105/22 and Corr. 1), New York,
    1964.

Satellite Communications: An Indian Study (A/AC.105/36), New York,
    1967.

Review of the Activities and Resources of the United Nations, of its
    Specialized Agencies and of Other Competent International Bodies
    Relating to the Peaceful Uses of Outer Space (A/AC.105/77), New
    York, 1970.

Review of National and Co-operative International Space Activities.
    Note by the Secretariat (A/AC.105/L.51 and Add. 1-6), New York,
    1970.

Report of the Secretary-General on Coordination of Secretariat Activities
    in the Field of Outer Space (A/AC.105/L.55), New York, 1970.

Review of the Activities and Resources of the United Nations, of its
    Specialized Agencies and of Other Competent International Bodies
    Relating to the Peaceful Uses of Outer Space (A/AC.105/C.1/L.34),
    New York, 1971.

Review of National and Co-operative International Space Activities for
    the Calendar Year 1970. Note by the Secretariat (A/AC.105/L.60
    and Add. 1-5 and Corr. 1), New York, 1971.

Review of National and Co-operative International Space Activities for
    the Calendar Year 1971. Note by the Secretariat (A/AC.105/L.64
    and Add. 1-4.) New York, 1972.

Draft Declaration of Guiding Principles on the Use of Satellite Broad-
    casting for the Free Flow of Information, the Spread of Education
    and Greater Cultural Exchange. Note by the Secretariat, (A/AC.
    105/104), New York, 1972.

Areas of Possible Future Interests and Orderly Consideration by the
    Committee on the Peaceful Uses of Outer Space and its Subsidiary
    Bodies. Working Paper submitted by the Government of Italy (A/AC.
    105/108), New York, 1972.

UNESCO Declaration of Guiding Principles on the Use of Satellite Broad-
    casting for the Free Flow of Information, the Spread of Education
    and Greater Cultural Exchange (A/AC.105/109 and Corr. 1), New
    York, 1973.

Review of National and Co-operative International Space Activities for
    the Calendar Year 1972. Note by the Secretariat (A/AC.105/L.68
    and Add. 1-4), New York, 1973.

Report of the United Nations Panel Meeting in India on Satellite Instruc-
    tional Television Systems (Delhi, 12-16 December; Ahmedabad,
    18-20 December 1972) (A/AC.105/114), New York, 1973.

Direct Broadcast Satellites. Working Paper Presented by the United
    States (A/AC.105/L.71), New York, 1973.

United Nations/UNESCO African Regional Seminar on Satellite Broad-
    casting Systems for Education and Development (Addis Ababa,
    October 1973) (A/AC.105/120), New York, 1973.

Review of National and Co-operative International Space Activities for
    the Calendar Year 1973. Note by the Secretariat (A/AC.105/125
    and Add. 1-5), New York, 1974.

Report of the United Nations Panel Meeting on Satellite Broadcasting
    Systems for Education, Tokyo, February-March 1974 (A/AC.105/
    128), New York, 1974.

                Subcommittees of the Committee on The Peaceful
                        Uses of Outer Space

Working Group on Direct Broadcast Satellites

Broadcasting from Satellites. Working Paper submitted by Canada and
    Sweden to the Working Group on Direct Broadcast Satellites (A/AC.
    105/49), New York, 1969.

Broadcasting-Satellite Service: Technical Considerations. Working
    Paper submitted to the Working Group on Direct Broadcast Satel-
    lites by the United States Delegation (A/AC.105/50), New York,
    1969.

Report of the Working Group on Direct Broadcast Satellites. (A/AC.105/
    51), New York, 1969.

Statement of the International Telecommunication Union (ITU) on Direct Broadcast Satellites (A/AC.105/52), New York, 1969.

Broadcasting from Satellites. Working Paper submitted by France to the Working Group on Direct Broadcast Satellites (A/AC.105/53), New York, 1969.

Broadcasting from Satellites. Working Paper submitted to the Working Group on Direct Broadcast Satellites by the Australian Delegation (A/AC.105/56), New York, 1969.

Geostatic Satellites—Prospective Use for Broadcasting of Television Programmes in Europe. Working Paper submitted to the Working Group on Direct Broadcast Satellites by the Italian Delegation (A/AC.105/57), New York, 1969.

Broadcasting from Satellites. Working Paper submitted by Canada and Sweden to the Second Session of the Working Group on Direct Broadcast Satellites (A/AC.105/59), New York, 1969.

Direct Broadcasting by Satellite: The Implications for UNESCO's Programme. Working Paper submitted to the Second Session of the Working Group on Direct Broadcast Satellites by the UNESCO Secretariat (A/AC.105/60), New York, 1969.

Direct Broadcast Satellites. Working Paper submitted to the Second Session of the Working Group on Direct Broadcast Satellites by the Czechoslovak Delegation (A/AC.105/61), New York, 1969.

Broadcasting from Satellites. Working Paper submitted by France to the Second Session of the Working Group on Direct Broadcast Satellites (A/AC.105/62), New York, 1969.

Broadcasting from Satellites. Working Paper submitted by Australia to the Second Session of the Working Group on Direct Broadcast Satellites (A/AC.105/63), New York, 1969.

Broadcasting from Satellites. Working Paper submitted by Mexico to the Second Session of the Working Group on Direct Broadcast Satellites (A/AC.105/64), New York, 1969.

Broadcasting from Satellites. Working Paper submitted to the Working Group on Direct Broadcast Satellites by the United Kingdom Delegation (A/AC.105/65), New York, 1969.

Report of the Second Session of the Working Group on Direct Broadcast Satellites (A/AC.105/66 and Corr. 1-2), New York, 1969.

Legal Problems Arising from Direct Broadcasts from Satellites (A/AC.105/
    WG.3/WP.1), New York, 1969.

Direct Broadcast Satellites. Working Paper presented by Canada and
    Sweden (A/AC.105/WG.3/L.1), New York, 1970.

Reports of the Working Group on Direct Broadcast Satellites: Comments
    Received from Governments, Specialized Agencies and Other Com-
    petent International Bodies (A/AC.105/79), New York, 1970.

Paper Presented by the Delegation of the Union of Soviet Socialist Re-
    publics to the Working Group on Direct Broadcast Satellites (A/AC.
    105/WG.3/CRP.1), New York, 1970.

Paper Presented by the Delegation of France to the Working Group on
    Direct Broadcast Satellites (A/AC.105/WG.3/CRP.2), New York,
    1970.

Report of the Working Group on Direct Broadcast Satellites on its Third
    Session (A/AC.105/83), New York, 1970.

Direct Broadcast Satellites. Working Paper presented by Canada and
    Sweden (A.AC.105/WG.3/L.5), New York, 1973.

Report by the United Nations Educational, Scientific and Cultural Organ-
    ization (A/AC.105/WG.3/L.5), New York, 1973.

Report of the Working Group on Direct Broadcast Satellites of the Work
    of its Fourth Session (A/AC.105/117), New York, 1973.

Principles Governing the Use by States of Artificial Earth Satellites for
    Direct Television Broadcasting. Prepared Pursuant to General
    Assembly Resolution 2916 (XXVII) with a View to Conclusion of an
    International Agreement or Agreements (A/AC.105/WG.3/V/CRP.1
    and Corr. 1), New York, 1974.

Direct Broadcast Satellites. Working Paper Presented by the United
    States (A/AC.105/WG.3 (V) CRP.2), New York, 1974.

Direct Broadcasting by Satellite. Working Paper Presented by the
    Delegation of Argentina (A/AC.105/WG.3 (V) CRP.3), New York,
    1974.

Report of the Working Group on Direct Broadcast Satellites on the Work
    of its Fifth Session (A/AC.105/127), New York, 1974.

Legal Subcommittee

Report of the Legal Sub-Committee on the Work of its Fifth Session
    (July-August and September 1966) (A/AC.105/35), New York,
    1966.

Report of the Legal Sub-Committee on the Work of its Sixth Session
    (June-July 1967) (A/AC.105/37), New York, 1967.

Report of the Legal Sub-Committee on the Work of its Special Session
    (December 1967) (A/AC.105/43), New York, 1967.

Report of the Legal Sub-Committee on the Work of its Seventh Session
    (June 1968) (A/AC.105/45), New York, 1968.

Report of the Legal Sub-Committee on the Work of its Eighth Session
    (June-July 1969) (A/AC.105/58), New York, 1969.

Report of the Legal Sub-Committee on the Work of its Ninth Session
    (June-July 1970) (A/AC.105/85), New York, 1970.

The Question of the Definition and/or the Delimitation of Outer Space
    (A/AC.105/C.2/7), New York, 1970.

Report of the Legal Sub-Committee on the Work of its Tenth Session
    (June-July 1971) (A/AC.105/94), New York, 1971.

Report of the Legal Sub-Committee on the Work of its Eleventh Session
    (April-May 1972). (A/AC.105/101), New York, 1972.

Report of the Legal Sub-Committee on the Work of its Twelfth Session
    (March-April 1973) (A/AC.105/115), New York, 1973.

Report of the Legal Sub-Committee on the Work of its Thirteenth Session
    (May 1974) (A/AC.105/133), New York, 1974.

Report of the Legal Sub-Committee on the Work of its Fourteenth Session
    (February-March 1975) (A/AC.105/147), New York, 1975.

UNPUBLISHED PAPERS

Cocca, Aldo Armando. "Regional Broadcast Agreements in the Americas."
    Paper presented to the Seminar on Direct Broadcasting by Satellite,
    sponsored by the American Society of International Law and the
    International Broadcast Institute, Bellagio, Italy, February 20-24,
    1974.

Galloway, Eilene. "Direct Broadcast Satellites." Paper presented to
the 17th Colloquium on the Law of Outer Space, September 30-
October 5, 1975, Amsterdam, Holland.

Gehrig, James J. "Broadcasting Satellites—Prospects and Problems."
Paper presented at the 17th Colloquium on the Law of Outer Space,
September 30-October 5, 1974, Amsterdam, Holland.

Kiss, Alexandre Ch. "Direct Broadcast Satellites and State Sovereignty."
Paper presented to the Seminar on Direct Broadcasting by Satellite,
sponsored by the American Society of International Law and the
International Broadcast Institute, Bellagio, Italy, February 20-24,
1974.

Kolosov, Y. M. "Direct Television Broadcasting Via Satellites as New
Medium of Mass Information." Paper presented to the Seminar on
Direct Broadcasting by Satellite, sponsored by the American Society
of International Law and the International Broadcast Institute,
Bellagio, Italy, February 20-24, 1974.

Paterman, Christian. "The Legal Problems of Spill-Over." Paper
presented to the Seminar on Direct Broadcasting by Satellite,
sponsored by the American Society of International Law and the
International Broadcast Institute, Bellagio, Italy, February 20-
24, 1974.

Rigalt, Antonio Francoz. "Urgency of a Draft Convention on Principles
Governing Direct Television Broadcasting by Satellites." Paper
prepared for the International Broadcast Institue General Meeting,
1974. Mexico City, September 1-5, 1974.

Smith, Delbert. "A Cage Full of Mirrors: Reflections on Communication
Satellites." Paper presented to the International Broadcast Institute
General Meeting, 1974. Mexico City, September 1-5, 1974.

Unga Filosofer. "Speeches Given at the Seminar on Cultural Imperialism." Stockholm, October 1974.

Vasquez, Modesto Seara. "Direct Broadcast Satellites and the Law."
Paper presented to the International Broadcast Institute General
Meeting, 1974, Mexico City, September 1-5, 1974.

Dissertations

Shafey, Sohair Borkat. "International Broadcasting and Its Societal
     Environments: A Test of a Hypothesis." Ph.D. dissertation,
     University of Southern California, 1970.

Erik. N. Valters, "International Law of Communications Satellites:
     Scarce Resources in a New Environment." Ph.D. dissertation,
     Columbia University, 1970.

ABOUT THE AUTHOR

BENNO SIGNITZER is a University Assistant and lecturer at the Department of Mass Communications ("Institut für Publizistik und Kommunikations-theorie"), University of Salzburg, Austria.

He is publishing articles in American, German, and Austrian professional and scholarly journals. While maintaining his interest in international and comparative aspects of mass communications, he is presently working on a comprehensive "Report on the Situation of the mass Media in Austria."

Dr. Signitzer is a graduate of the University of Salzburg Law School where he was awarded an Austrian Dr. juris degree in 1971. After studies of mass communications in France he was granted a Fulbright scholarship to complete his postgraduate education in the United States. He received his M.A. and Ph.D. degrees in Speech-Communication from Bowling Green State University.

BROADCASTING TO THE SOVIET UNION:
International Politics and Radio
                    Maury Lisann

EDUCATIONAL TELEVISION FOR DEVELOPING
COUNTRIES: A Policy Critique and Guide
                    edited by Robert F. Arnove

FOREIGN AFFAIRS NEWS AND THE BROADCAST
JOURNALIST
                    Robert M. Batscha

INTERNATIONAL COMMERCIAL SATELLITE
COMMUNICATIONS: Economic and Political Issues
of the First Decade of INTELSAT
                    Marcellus S. Snow

MASS COMMUNICATION AND CONFLICT RESOLUTION:
The Role of the Information Media in the Advancement
of International Understanding
                    W. Phillips Davison

MASS COMMUNICATION RESEARCH: Major Issues
and Future Directions*
                    edited by W. Phillips Davison
                    and Frederick T. C. Yu

THE ROLE OF COMMUNICATIONS IN THE MIDDLE
EAST CONFLICT: Ideological and Religious Aspects
                    Yonah Alexander

*Also available in paperback as a PSS Student Edition.